Looking Back from the Wild Side

by CJ Anderson

TEACH Services, Inc.
P U B L I S H I N G
www.TEACHServices.com • (800) 367-1844

World rights reserved. This book or any portion thereof may not be copied or reproduced in any form or manner whatever, except as provided by law, without the written permission of the publisher, except by a reviewer who may quote brief passages in a review.

The author assumes full responsibility for the accuracy of all facts and quotations as cited in this book. The opinions expressed in this book are the author's personal views and interpretations, and do not necessarily reflect those of the publisher.

This book is provided with the understanding that the publisher is not engaged in giving spiritual, legal, medical, or other professional advice. If authoritative advice is needed, the reader should seek the counsel of a competent professional.

Copyright © 2020 CJ Anderson

Copyright © 2020 TEACH Services, Inc.

ISBN-13: 978-1-4796-0751-8 (Paperback)

ISBN-13: 978-1-4796-1194-2 (ePub)

Library of Congress Control Number: 2020915626

All Scripture quotations, unless otherwise indicated, are taken from the New King James Version®. Copyright © 1990 by Thomas Nelson. Used by permission. All rights reserved.

Figure 1: *Our logo shows our view to the south with Two Tail Mountain in the foreground and Katka Mountain in the background. Our pond to the northwest abounds with cattails.*

Table of Contents

Acknowledgements. 9
Introduction   Looking Back from the Wild Side. 11
Chapter 1 The "P" Word 13
Chapter 2 Getting More for Your College Tuition. 17
Chapter 3 Wigg's Meadow and Other Adventures. 23
Chapter 4 AZ 4 Me. 29
Chapter 5 Everyone Needs a Big Brother. 33
Chapter 6 "Spud" the Wonder Dog. 38
Chapter 7 "Adventure Club" 42
Chapter 8 The Big Bike Trip. 48
Chapter 9 Horses, Horses. 58
Chapter 10 Practice Kids 64
Chapter 10 Camping 101 72
Chapter 12 What's So Grand About that Canyon? 77
Chapter 13 Motorcycles Aren't for Sissies 81
Chapter 14 Mexico or Bust. 86
Chapter 15 "The" Boat 90
Chapter 16 Turnabout's Fair Play—Isn't It?. 96
Chapter 17 Tales from a Kitchen 101
Chapter 18 A Song for Your Heart 107
Conclusion. 111

***Figure* 2:** *Kattail Glyn as seen from Two Tail Mountain.*

Acknowledgements

To my husband, Rob, and our children, Eric and Scot, who made most of these adventures possible and who helped me find the brighter side of life. To all my friends who encouraged me to write and to all who will read these pages. May they help you find the brighter side of a sometimes dark and discouraging world and may they also help remind you that God will never leave you nor forsake you.

Introduction

Looking Back from the Wild Side

My husband and I lived on forty acres in an area of Idaho full of animals that I had never seen while growing up except in a zoo or in a book. Many of them were bigger than I was and never smiled or trimmed their nails. This may have had something to do with their dispositions and may have contributed to a very active food chain. A bit of humor or even a smile might not have gone a long way in impressing the wildlife, but I'm quite sure that a simple smile can change a person's entire day. I hope you will find these stories from my life funny enough to put a smile on your face so that your own Christian walk may make folks want to know more about the Jesus you love!

Animal pictures were taken from our porch at Kattail Glyn. The name Kattail Glyn is descriptive in that Kat is taken from Katka Mountain and Tail from Two Tail Mountain, both of which can be seen from our front porch. By definition, a glen or glyn is a mountain meadow. So it was that our home place became known as Kattail Glyn. "Be still, and know that I *am* God" the Bible says in Psalm 46:10. It is so still and quiet there that at times you could hear your own heart beating. Search for your own quiet place to reflect on God's leading in your life or come sit a spell with us on our porch and be refreshed.

Figure 3: *That animal trail through the woods, aka our driveway.*

"I will make a covenant of peace with them, and cause wild beasts to cease from the land; and they will dwell safely in the wilderness and sleep in the woods" (Ezekiel 34:25).

Chapter 1
The "P" Word

In our family, four letter words of ill repute include p-l-a-n. It is an utterance bulging with doom and gloom, guaranteed to jinx any intended outing with delay, breakage, accident, injury, incredible unpredicted weather conditions or perhaps a combination of all the aforementioned. Uttered in the presence of any of our clan, you can depend on reactions ranging from raised eyebrows to gasps.

While we try desperately to avoid the word "plan," it occasionally slips in unnoticed. For example, not so very long ago our kids asked us to come help them build a new home. Our church family innocently asked when we "planned" to return. Not even noticing how the word had slipped into the conversation, we assured them we wouldn't be gone more than a month, perhaps six weeks at the very most. That was the beginning of our latest "planned" episode. What most people fail to understand is that p-l-a-n not only seems to jinx us, but it slithers around and about and attaches itself to everyone within slithering range.

Our kids were ready for us to start work as soon as we arrived, but they hadn't accounted for any "slithering." We were about to begin our very own two-week version of the movie "Groundhog Day." For the next four months, no matter what the question, the answer was always the same: "About two weeks." When will the plumbers be finished? "About two weeks." When can we begin the electrical? "About two weeks." Can we start painting now? "In about two weeks." When is supper? "In about two weeks." Believe me, I've learned that "about two weeks" is not a very satisfying answer to any question!

Our kids probably would never have asked us to come help them if they had known we had been asked when we "planned" to return. That one question, all by itself, set back the completion date of their home by months. That may sound preposterous to you but, believe me, I've had a lot of experience with this sort of thing. After about three months of mostly sweeping and picking up other contractor's messes, we decided we had better get home. The house wasn't finished but winter in northern Idaho was getting serious and the state of Idaho was getting ready to swear out a warrant if I didn't show up for jury duty. That's when the weather kicked in. There are a number of routes you can drive to get from southeastern Tennessee to northern Idaho, but that one fateful word slithered around the country until there wasn't a single route home that wasn't fraught with snow, sleet, ice, avalanches, flooding or mudslides. Go figure.

After about five months, the house was finally completed and there appeared to be a small window in the weather that we could slip through to get home. That's when someone else who knew about our home in northern Idaho, and the many projects we had waiting for us there, asked the fateful question. What are you "planning" to do when you get home? Ach! Well, not in my wildest imaginings was I "planning" on what we found when we got home.

For starters, there was a berm of snow about six feet high and ten feet across in front of our driveway. We came armed with shovels and a pair of snowshoes and started right in shoveling. After about an hour, we had a small path almost one-third of the way through the berm. Realizing that spring would probably arrive before we finished shoveling, we started down the half-mile driveway on snowshoes. Breaking trail in four feet of powder snow is something I outgrew about fifty years ago. If we could just get into the house, we would be able to get a fire started in the wood stove and start thawing things out. In retrospect, we might have been better served if we had started the fire in the living room instead of the wood stove. The short version of this noble endeavor was that six days later, we were able to drive to our home and unpack.

Upon entering the house for the first time, we noticed that someone or something had been busy changing our décor. There were now small, dark, oblong-shaped dots over, upon and in everything. Spring cleaning, at least in January, hadn't exactly been at the top of my to-do list. However, it looked like that would have to change. It was about that time when we discovered that the pipes had frozen and some of the plumbing fixtures had broken. I went to get some bottled water from the refrigerator and had opened the refrigerator door only a crack when I made another startling discovery. Somehow, the refrigerator had gotten turned off and the substance of the odor of about four months of rotted food came oozing out into the room. Believe me, even your imagination won't be able to compete with that reality.

We were worried about all the snow on the roof. My husband and I were both retirement age and felt a bit of trepidation with regard to crawling out on a snow-covered metal roof. Snowboarding experience should be a prerequisite for this activity. We contacted a friend who agreed to help us and soon learned that two of our three chimneys had been sheared off by some of the snow that had managed to slide down the roof. The snow was so much deeper than the diverters that it just went over the top of them. Because the house was our priority, we weren't able to get the carport roof cleared before one side of it broke down from the weight of the snow.

> *My husband and I were both retirement age and felt a bit of trepidation with regard to crawling out on a snow-covered metal roof. Snowboarding experience should be a prerequisite for this activity.*

About this time, we were thinking that, while it might be early to drop back in on our son and his wife in Tennessee, surely our other son and daughter-in-law in sunny Southern California must be longing to see the parents. It was, after all, less than five months before spring, so surely he and his wife could tolerate us that long if our Tennessee kin could. We made the fateful "if just one more thing happens" declaration and sure enough, things began to settle down, the sun came out and our mood began to brighten.

I listened intently for the "p" word and began to relax as I realized there was not even a hint of slithering in sight. However, in my sixty-plus years, I have learned that life is not static. Somehow, without even a hint of planning, we managed to wreck our truck. Then, coming home a few nights later, late at night, we encountered a large propane delivery truck stuck fast in what we affectionately call our driveway, but which most other people refer to as "that animal trail through the woods." The driver had long since abandoned his rig along with the prospect of freezing to death for what I'm sure he considered a better option: an eleven mile hike into town that might only cost him a toe or two, unless of course, he got eaten by a mountain lion or trampled to death by a herd of elk. As for us, we only had to worry about the elk or an occasional cougar as we hiked the half-mile into our place in the darkness of the night.

So you see, our lives are fraught with more than your average calamities as we seek to dodge the fate of the "p" word. Oh, and by the way, you might want to try chocolate chips for your next extermination project. The mice in our house ate two large bags of the things—right down to the last morsel and we haven't seen or heard from them since!

Chapter 2

Getting More for Your College Tuition

About a hundred years ago, when I was in college, I found myself rooming with two other freshmen and a sophomore in an ancient, run-down apartment complex serving as an overflow for the dorms. The idea was to put two upperclassmen in charge of two underclassmen and hope the whole place didn't self-destruct. I guess we were the leftovers because our apartment ended up with three freshmen and one sophomore and nary an upperclassman ever darkened our door. While I did go to college to get a taste of "higher education" (it would be seventeen years before I would actually finish), I never turned down an opportunity to participate in extra-curricular activities—kind of a value-added plan.

> *One of my roommates was from Texas and I don't know if that had anything to do with the fact that she was mortally afraid of mice or not*

One of my roommates was from Texas and I don't know if that had anything to do with the fact that she was mortally afraid of mice or not. The truth was that she was a bundle of entertainment anytime I could produce anything that remotely resembled a mouse—living or dead. Even though we were satellite occupants, the dorm always included us in their parties and celebrations—as well as all other gatherings of not such jocular content. The Christmas party was to be an opportunity for the "secret sis" program to get a little publicity and all the girls were to provide a gift as an unknown benefactor. Just think of the potential—no one was even supposed to know where the stuff came from! Well, I certainly couldn't pass up that opportunity. I obtained a freshly demised mouse from the broom shop where I worked. I wrapped it in plastic and put it into an old perfume box that I rigged with a spring so that upon opening the box the contents would become airborne.

I thought it best not to attend the party in case there might be any finger-pointing, but I heard later that the whole caper was a smashing success. The girls were all seated on the floor around the Christmas tree and a few girls at a time would open their presents. When my roommate opened her gift, she became the focal point of the entire party. I guess it doesn't matter whether you know what a thing is when it's flying toward you and the previous point of occupancy is all sound and animation—you just start screaming and get rid of the thing. Some things seem to take longer than they actually do, but I really don't think it took all that long for that poor little dead creature to make its way to the edge of the crowd where it was finally positively identified and disposed of. Luckily, some folks have a sense of humor and when the supposed danger was past, a few chuckles finally turned into chortles, then elevated to open laughter and finally the laughter overcame the finger-pointing.

Another roommate came from Minnesota. A lot of people associate that state with chill and cold, but my roommate was warm and bubbly with long, fiery-red hair. No one even thought about cold when she was around. I must digress here to tell you that in college, you will eat anything—eventually. So, when my grandmother sent some exotic jams, stuff she didn't like, like guava and mint and such, we simply put it on a shelf for some future moment of near starvation.

One day, as I opened a cupboard, I noticed my Minnesota roommate's wave set sitting right next to the mint jelly. What do you know, they were the same color! You must keep in mind the antiquity of this occurrence—long ago when girls rolled their hair in a nightly ritual of pain and suffering in order to produce a few curls to attract the attention of the opposite sex. I decided a little extra time spent on an unassigned science project might prove entertaining as well as enlightening. Besides, you never know when some lonely, young, aspiring scientist might add to the bank of scientific information—besides, no one else was around.

The mint jelly was mixed with a bit of water and put in the wave set bottle. The unrinsed jelly jar was filled with the wave set. Now, either my roommates would eat the wave set or set their hair with the jelly! I waited for results patiently at first, but after a while the waiting got boring and I simply forgot about the whole thing.

Weeks later, during exam week, I awoke one morning to strange utterances coming from the semi-darkness. My roommate with the long, fiery-red hair had stayed up late studying the night before and had washed and set her hair—with the mint jelly! This turned out to be much more scientific than one might imagine because who knew that sugar, being an organic substance, would absorb into each individual hair strand and couldn't be readily washed out? When the rest of us woke up, at least three out of the four people began to laugh. (Just a little statistics thrown in for good measure—see how this whole value-added education thing works?)

Accusations about Elmer's Glue were soon put to rest, but one could easily see how she jumped to such an outrageous conclusion. Instead of her hair falling loosely curled about her shoulders, as it normally would have, her hair still looked like all the rollers were still in place. Five shampoos, sets and dries later, her hair began to take on more normal attributes, but by then, she had missed all her exams. The day had slowly passed as she had to interrupt her hair salon activities to go first to her work supervisor, then to each of her four professors to let them know she had extenuating circumstances that prevented her from attendance. Upon hearing her tale, they would pull her headscarf from her very stiff circlets of hair, give them a solid pat, then start with a nice smile and end up in gales of laughter. This would draw the attention of any students within range and they too would join the cacophony. Even with all the encouragement I could give her, my poor roommate just didn't seem to gain much pleasure from bringing smiles to the otherwise stressed and tired faces of her fellow classmates.

Well, some of the best ideas are spontaneous and this brings us to the third roommate. Roommate number three fancied herself far and above us lowly freshmen since she was, after all, not only a sophomore, but the only female student above freshman status that was willing to take on the job of shepherding three freshmen through the perils of their first year of higher education. Her greatest problem was that the three of us highly resented the whole idea of being shepherded. Following close on the heels of that problem was the fact that she had been given upperclassman privileges because of her shepherding attempts. Reminding the rest of us of her obvious greater maturity was one of her greater pleasures. My uncle taught at the college I attended. His family, consisting of my aunt and two small cousins, lived nearby. I kept my dog at their place and one day, upon returning to my room, I realized I had forgotten to give all the dog treats to my pet. They were round affairs of various colors and had a certain attractiveness about them. Roommate number three was just getting ready to leave when a scathingly brilliant and spontaneous idea occurred to me.

> *She popped that dog biscuit into her mouth as I watched intently. She began to make strange faces as she chewed. When she got to the point that I was afraid she would spit it out, I said, "Oh, I forgot to tell you. You're not supposed to chew it. You're supposed to suck on it."*

"Say," I said, "my little cousins gave me some of their candy to share with my roommates." "No thanks," she replied, "I'm just on my way out and don't really think I care for any." "That's really too bad. You know it's tough for little kids to share sometimes, especially if it's something they really like. They'll want to know how you liked the candy," I said. "Well, OK then," my roommate said, "I guess it won't hurt to have just one piece."

She popped that dog biscuit into her mouth as I watched intently. She began to make strange faces as she chewed. When she got to the point that I was afraid she would spit it out, I said, "Oh, I forgot to tell you. You're not supposed to chew it. You're supposed to suck on it."

She actually made a feeble attempt at sucking on the somewhat mangled dog biscuit but by then she was losing interest in the feelings of my two small cousins. Anyway, I just couldn't hold in my own bursting humor anymore. It turns out she was pretty proud of being a fourth-generation vegetarian and not very appreciative of my concerns over her lack of protein.

It wasn't long after this episode that somehow the dorm found room for one more student to squeeze in. Funny how there hadn't been any room before but, on the bright side, I now had a whole wing of girls to help make sure I could get a full-value education from my tuition fees.

Figure 4: *An early spring herd of elk in the meadow.*

Chapter 3
Wigg's Meadow and Other Adventures

In our family, an adventure is anything you live to tell about. My husband was teaching in a university in Tennessee and our two sons were in elementary school. I was nearing the end of my seventeen-year quest for a college degree and had heard tales from other students about an uncommonly beautiful place called Wigg's Meadow. It was supposed to be a long, sweeping meadow of tall grasses surrounded by 360° of mountain peaks.

Another family that we often shared adventures with had two daughters close to the ages of our sons. We called them to see if they would like to share a picnic with us at Wigg's Meadow and they readily agreed. It was a summer day, full of sunshine and promise. Granted, the directions I had received were a bit sketchy, but surely a place of such great beauty couldn't be that hard to find. We had given ourselves plenty of time to find the place and still enjoy a timely lunch, but the afternoon wore on and we still hadn't found it. Our kids began to get cranky. That was a minor irritation compared to the adults who started to roll their eyes and throw around sarcastic remarks about my ancestors and how they ever found America. It was nearing time for supper when the hunt was called off and we looked for any spot flat enough to stop and devour our belated lunch.

After that, just about every weekend was spent in the pursuit of Wigg's Meadow. Sometimes the forest trails that served as roads got so bad we'd stop the car and proceed on foot. A few times on the way back to the car, we'd find bear prints in the path that hadn't been there when we'd started our trek. Eventually, we'd give up—again. Back at school the next week, I'd ask for better directions. Funny, but no one who had ever been there was willing to take the time to show us where this elusive place was.

Finally, one weekend about three months and four states later, I was pretty sure that we had found the right trail to Wigg's Meadow. Darkness had begun to creep up the hollows and everyone suddenly began to remember pressing engagements that would require their immediate return home. We had to be close, but I just couldn't get them to go any farther. Several more weekends passed before we were able to continue our search and by that time our friends seemed to have lost interest in their pioneering pursuits. It took a lot of effort, but they finally succumbed to our coaxing and agreed to go just one more time.

When we picked them up, the girls were acting all pouty. It seems their mom was making them wear winter jackets, hats, gloves, boots—the whole nine yards and it wasn't even winter yet. Our boys didn't help their mood any since they only had to wear their light jackets and tennis shoes. I had to get after the boys a time or two for teasing the girls, even though I agreed that the girls did look a bit silly under all those wraps. Granted, it was mid-October, but the sun was shining and we were sure to find the place this time.

We drove until we ran out of trail, parked the car and headed out on foot. We decided to leave the food in the car until we could scout the place out. Just as the trail broke out from the trees, there it was! Just like in the "Sound of Music" we all ran up the meadow. It was glorious! We twirled around to take in the majesty, but what was that? As our twirl completed its 360th degree, the mountains that had just been there seconds ago weren't anymore. We all just stood there for a few minutes in silence trying to take in what had just happened. Suddenly, I shouted out that I knew what had happened to the mountains and that we'd better get back to the car—NOW! By this time in our adventure, people weren't paying that much attention to my suggestions anymore, but it took just another minute or two for the reality of plummeting temperatures to let everyone know of the oncoming blizzard. Moments later, the snow began to swirl about. It might have been considered beautiful had it not been for the chattering teeth of my offspring who were becoming increasingly difficult to see in the white. That's when my friend began peeling layers off her own offspring to share with our boys. No one worried about color or style. We just knew we had to get them warm. We hurried as fast as we could on the slippery trail back to the car where we could all be warm. As we came

Chapter 3 Wigg's Meadow and Other Adventures

down the mountain, the snow changed to rain and we did the best imitation of a picnic that we could while driving home.

Over the years, Wigg's Meadow has occasionally come up in conversation, but not one of our expedition suggested a return. Some folks that have overheard us talking about Wigg's Meadow have shown a bit of curiosity as to the whereabouts of the place. Any of us are happy to provide sketchy directions, but always decline an invitation to be a guide!

It took some time before our friends were ready for another adventure, but one day they called to invite us to go with them to the water slide park. We had planned to go canoeing that day and assured them that we could probably fit in both activities if they would be willing to go canoeing first. We had two canoes so that would make two adults, two kids and one dog in each canoe.

We headed out to find North Chickamauga Creek, a place we had looked up in a "things to do" type publication. What they had failed to list in their publication was all the things we were going to get to do besides paddling. We put in at the assigned point. It was a quiet stream, gently meandering through giant leafy trees. We had gone about a mile when we came to one of those giant leafy trees that had fallen across the quiet stream. The banks were high, steep and muddy at this point and there was nothing to do but go alongside the massive trunk, crawl out onto it, pull the canoe up and over it, then load everybody and everything back into the canoe. I bother to detail this process because it will save me time typing and you reading if from this point on, I simply refer to this process as doing "the thing again."

We paddled on downstream for about another mile having to do "the thing again" only ten or twelve more times. Along about this point, the troops requested a conference so we huddled on one of the logs to decide whether we should go on or turn back. Surely, we must be near the end of the endless portaging and should continue on. Certainly, we were hot, sweaty, tired and muddy, but to admit defeat now would surely seem cowardly—at least that's something like what I had to say to muster the troops. Besides, it couldn't be much farther, and we still had the water slide to look forward to—cool, refreshing and CLEAN! The prospects of backtracking and doing "the thing again" finally won out and on downstream we went.

Shortly, the waterway opened up and there appeared to be no fallen trees in sight. I was in the process of assuring the troops that they had indeed made the right decision when suddenly all my laud and praise was drowned out by loud moans. Rounding a bend, we saw what looked like a sawmill yard after a tornado. There were so many crisscrossed, downed trees we couldn't even put the canoe into the stream between trees. "The thing again" took on a whole new process. Keeping kids and dogs from slipping between trees down into the murky water was our main objective and any forward progress we made was considered a bonus.

We couldn't have come all that far, but turning back now was out of the question. While we hadn't covered much distance, we'd used up *a lot* of time. We hoped to be able to classify this as an adventure, but so far there just wasn't that much evidence that we—at least the me part of we—were going to live to tell about it.

Lucky for us, summer days are long and we actually made it to the place we had left our cars. Of course, by this time it was too late to go to the promised water slide, and besides, we were now not only hot, sweaty, tired and muddy, but hungry and cranky as well. Better save the water slide for another time.

We called our friends one day some time later to see if they were still planning to go to the water slide. They said only if there was no adventure involved. I said it was after all a public recreational attraction and I didn't see how there could be any adventure involved in sliding down a tube into a pool of sanitary water. So, putting the whole North Chickamauga Creek thing behind us, off we all went to enjoy a day at the water slide park.

Everything probably would have been fine if it weren't for my great concern for others. After all, if you are going to spend all that money for an afternoon of fun, you really want to make sure everyone is having fun. So, after a couple of slides down to acquaint ourselves with the possibilities, I suggested we make a train by going down all together, one behind the other. I didn't figure it needed a lot of explanation. After all, it seemed everyone should know that once we hit the pool—well, you know.

My friend wanted to be first, I guess she figured that she could look out after all of us that way, so I went after her, our husbands next and then the kids. Oh, what a magnificent train we made! We were all laughing and shouting on the way down—definitely getting our money's worth—until we rounded the last turn and splashed into the pool. Either my friend hadn't figured out how to get out of the way or just didn't do it fast enough, but one after another she was mowed over by the various parts of the train. Actually, she provided a kind of skid whereby each one of us would bounce off from her, thus preventing bodily injury to any of the rest of the train.

It was noble of her to have such concern for us, but it did take quite a while for all her bruises to heal. I can verify that lack of oxygen will not prevent bruising. She managed to hold her breath all the time we were bouncing off from her. She does still talk to us and can even be occasionally talked into going places with us, but she seems to have developed a nervous condition in her later years that prevents her from taking part in any adventures.

Figure 5: *Coyote waiting for lunch.*

Chapter 4
AZ 4 Me

I was going to get one of those fancy vanity license plates that said "AZ4ME." Yep, I wanted everyone to know that Arizona was the place I'd rather be. But then, of course, that wasn't until just before we left Arizona.

My husband had been called to a teaching job at a boarding school in Scottsdale, Arizona. We arrived just at the beginning of July in our vehicle with the kind of air conditioning native Arizonans refer to as 250 air conditioning—that is to say two windows down and fifty miles an hour will condition the air so you can just about stand it. Our furniture hadn't arrived yet, which wasn't all bad since the house wasn't ready anyway. We had decided to spend the night in our camper—also not air-conditioned. About that time the principal of the school came by and informed us we'd be staying with his family until our house was ready. He said he didn't want to wake up the next morning and find us gone, which is what he was sure would happen if we didn't have air conditioning.

My first impression of Arizona was not much to write about—actually I cried and begged my husband to not make us stay in such an awful place. The principal's wife patted me on the shoulder and told me that by the time we had been there two years, we'd never want to leave. Also, she said that while the heat seemed pretty bad (hello, 113° is BAD!), it was a dry heat and not nearly as bad as it seemed. I figured the heat must have affected her brain for her to think it wasn't all that bad. At any rate, we did stay and so began our love affair with Arizona.

We had brought our canoes with us and decided to look on a map to find a place where there would be enough water to go canoeing. We found a big blue spot on the map that wasn't too far away and decided that would be a good place to start. We drove to the area and sure enough off in the distance we could see a large dam. We drove and drove, but no matter which road we took we could not seem to get to that dam. We finally decided to drive out through the desert and see if we could get to it that way.

After a bit, we came upon two men shooting guns. They had quite an arsenal of weaponry and I was thinking we were kind of vulnerable, but then since they might have a harder time shooting someone they were looking in the eye, we decided to stop. They were staring at us with such intent that I was beginning to wonder if they weren't more nervous than we were. I leaned out the window and ask one of the fellows how we might get to the other side of that dam. Never taking his eyes off the canoe tied to the top of our car, he asked why we wanted to get over there. I thought it was fairly obvious but proceeded to explain that we were looking for a place we could canoe. Still looking nervous, he said, "Well lady, you might as well put that canoe down right here because there is just as much water here as there is on the other side of that dam."

> *We were full of anticipation and couldn't wait to feel the coolness of the water. When we rounded the last bend before the lake, there was utter silence as we all just stared and stared at the place that had been a pristine lake such a short time before. Now there was only a tiny trickle way down in a deep valley with dried mud flats spreading out to what had once been a beautiful shoreline.*

We felt kind of silly, but surely not as silly as the people who built a dam in the middle of a desert. I wasn't sure we should stay for two years if the heat could affect one's judgment that much. We never could figure out what those fellows' problem was either, but someone later suggested that anyone driving around in the desert with a canoe on top of their vehicle was bound to be suspect.

We decided to try some other place and just before dark found a large lake (also in the middle of the desert, but at least these engineers had the foresight to check for water first). We took note of where this place was and determined to return there when we'd have more time to explore.

A few weeks later we rounded up our crew and headed out. We were full of anticipation and couldn't wait to feel the coolness of the water. When we rounded the last bend before the lake, there was utter silence as we all just stared and stared at the place that had been a pristine lake such a short time before. Now there was only a tiny trickle way down in a deep valley with dried mud flats spreading out to what had once been a beautiful shoreline. How could this be? Surely this was the right place. Where had all that water gone? Once again feeling kind of silly, we returned home in defeat.

I felt sorry for our canoes. OK, so that's silly too, but I took the hose when we got home and sprayed them with water. I told the neighbors I was washing them off, but the real reason was I didn't want them to forget what water felt like.

We gave up our quest and turned to the experts. We stopped in at a sporting goods store and asked about a location that might be suitable for canoeing. They gave us the location of another lake, but by now I had developed a fairly suspicious nature and wasn't going to be taken in so easily. I told them of our experience with the dam and detected a bit of a smirk as they told us it had been built for flood control, not water storage. Then I told them of our experience with the disappearing lake and their smirks turned into gales of laughter as they explained that the lake had been drained so the dam could be repaired. So, we took their word and sure enough found a lake with real water in it. Of course, everyone else had found it too and we spent most of the day dodging speed boats.

This whole water thing turned out to be quite a trial. The principal, still fearful we would either leave or get ourselves killed before the school year finished, told us that while it seldom rained there, we should get home as quickly as possible if it should even begin to sprinkle. He said the roads could flood and we would be unable to drive anywhere if we waited very long. Now, how silly is that. Sprinkles!

One night I wakened to the soft sound of raindrops. I laid there imagining the dog swimming around the backyard until curiosity got the best of me. I got out of bed for a look. Who would have believed all that water! It was inches from the house and there sitting forlornly on the only dry spot in the back yard, our back stoop, sat the dog! Maybe there was something to all this weather paranoia after all.

The next time it started to sprinkle, I suggested we run to the store for a few essentials, just in case we wouldn't be able to get to the store at all later, you know, just to be on the safe side. By the time we left the store, the way was blocked by floodwaters. We went another way, but that was blocked too. It was getting dark. Up ahead of us we could see taillights on the other side of a flooded area and thought maybe people were driving through it. That's when we noticed the car in the flooded area was moving backward, not forward, and had a line attached to it. It was pulled to high ground and someone walked over and opened the doors. Water gushed out and there sat four people, wet clear up to their chests. Alright then, trying to drive through might not be such a good idea.

We turned around and tried still another route. This time we were able to get to a main road and turn toward home. The road was flooded and the only way to tell if you were anywhere close to being on it was to stay in the middle of the telephone poles on either side. Since the road was highest in the middle, that was the shallowest part and a good place to be. We were making pretty good progress until a fire truck came along—also in the middle of the road. It didn't give any evidence that it intended to move over in the slightest—and it didn't. The wake it made went clear over our windshield and gave our engine a good dousing, bringing us to a standstill. There we sat, still dry on the inside but unable to open the doors. My husband and I took off our shoes and climbed out through the sunroof. Our eldest, a first-grader, steered the car while we pushed. We couldn't figure out if we were even on the paved road because it was all gravely under our feet. Against a very strong current, we managed to push the car far enough to get it out of the water and let it dry out so that it would start again. We finally made it home and later learned that the gravel we were pushing the car through was where the road had been washed away.

Our adventures in Arizona continued for many years and later, when our principal took a job in another state, I had the opportunity to give back some sage advice to his wife. "Don't worry about the cold in Colorado," I said, "It's a dry cold and won't be nearly as bad as you might think!" (He, he, he!)

Chapter 5
Everyone Needs a Big Brother

As a small child I lived an incredibly happy existence with my grandparents and an uncle named Dave who was just a year-and-a-half older than me. Dave was just like a big brother and I loved him dearly. I was his shadow and I'm sure that must have plagued him at times. Looking back, I can see that sometimes his actions were meant to leave me behind but I so adored him I never felt put off.

For reasons beyond my understanding, it was important to Dave that we should be tough and the toughest personages we knew about were Native Americans or "Indians" as we knew them then. So it was that Dave was often devising tests for us so we could be tough like the "Indians." The tests might be something as simple as running the sink full of hot water and seeing who could keep their hands in it the longest or running around our large country home barefoot in the snow. Even these simple tests could go awry—as the barefoot in the snow caper did—because we forgot to check the door and got locked out. Simply knocking on the door to be let back in was not an option because my grandparents did not encourage our efforts to become tough except as it pertained to our backsides. Dave and I took off our flannel shirts and stood around on them shivering in the cold as we moved from one window to the next until we found one we could pry open and go through to get back inside. More complex tests involved climbing and knot tying, and I can tell you I spent many afternoons either in high places I was afraid to come down out of or tied up in some remote corner of the basement or barn. To be fair, we would take turns, but I never mastered the art of knot tying while Dave could keep me out of his hair for an entire afternoon with his rope skills. I never worried too much, though, because I knew that come suppertime Dave would have to confess my whereabouts to my grandpa, and my grandpa would ALWAYS, without fail, come rescue me.

My grandmother did the auction and yard sale scene. Dave and I were her miniature stevedores and were allowed to keep some things after she had gone through the boxes. One time we found a strange machine that had two pads attached to wires that were hooked to a box that you could plug in. The box had a dial on it and you could increase the voltage impulses to the pads by turning the dials. This proved to be a wonderful test of toughness as the muscles involved in the pad placement would contract. You could really feel the hurt if you turned the dial up very high. We entertained ourselves for some time with this strange machine until we were both sore and ready to do something else. We decided to try the machine out on my grandmother's corner chair. We unzipped the cushion, put the pads in, and re-zipped it, then ran the wires behind the chair where we hid with the box until my grandmother came to take a rest. We weren't sure the pads would work inside the cushion so we turned the machine up all the way! And boy, did it work! I don't know how tough it made my grandmother, but I know that Dave and I both had the opportunity to have our backsides toughened up quite a bit! Oh, and by the time we had regained our composure, the machine had mysteriously disappeared, never to be seen again.

Probably the only time I ever got the best of Dave was the time he decided we would be tougher if we ate like the Indians and he was pretty sure the Indians ate their eggs raw. He took an egg from the fridge and shook and shook and shook it. Then he took a knife, whacked off the top of the egg, peered down into the shell at the still very round yolk and held it out for me to swallow. I shook my head and said, "You first." (I had never been so bold as to suggest such a thing before.)

"Oh, you are such a baby!" he said, as he swallowed the raw egg. He quickly grabbed another egg, whacked the top off and shoved it to me to swallow, but I was too focused on his changing color. "Here!" he said emphatically, but I just couldn't take my eyes off his face. Suddenly, he turned and bolted for the door. Outside, he relieved himself of the offending egg and most everything else he may have ingested that day and I never heard anything more about the Indians after that.

Chapter 5 Everyone Needs a Big Brother

We moved on to other adventures after our Indian phase. One Christmas our cousin Mike was visiting while we were living in town just a few blocks from the river. It was cold outside but we still didn't have any snow, so we were messing around inside getting under foot and generally just being a nuisance. The adults finally declared that we should go outside to wear off some energy but that we should stay away from the river. We bundled up and headed out. After wandering about town, without really meaning to, we found ourselves at the river. The river ran swift enough so as not to freeze in winter, and someone had left a raft tied out in the current. We pulled the raft in by its ropes and took turns holding the ropes while we jumped onto the raft then let go of the ropes and floated back out into the current. It was great fun and we spent the greater part of the afternoon letting our imaginations run wild as we drifted along in the river.

After a while Dave decided he wanted to go somewhere else and began pulling us to shore. We all jumped off the raft onto shore, but Mike changed his mind and decided he wanted to stay and play on the raft some more. Dave and I started away from the river but decided to watch and see if Mike could actually pull the raft in by himself. It was a struggle, but he managed to get it pulled in. The larger problem was that he could not hold the raft and jump at the same time so when he let go of the rope and jumped the raft moved faster than he anticipated and he jumped right into the river! Dave and I thought that was just about the funniest thing we had ever seen and were rolling on the ground laughing until we suddenly realized that Mike was nowhere to be seen. We ran to the river's edge and looked down and there was Mike, standing on the bottom of the river, under the water, out of our reach. Dave got down on his belly and hung over the embankment while I lay on the ground grasping his feet. From this position Dave could just barely reach Mike's upstretched hand and pull him ashore. Well, Mike could at least breathe now, but our problems were far from over. His clothing was quickly freezing and soon he could not even take a step. Dave and I carried him the several blocks uphill to the house but now what? If we took him in straight away we were all in for a good licking for going to the river and we were pretty sure our backsides were tough enough already. We opted to hang around a bit until the coast was clear and we could get him in the side door and down to the basement where we could stuff him between the furnace and the wall until he thawed out. Having successfully gotten Mike to the basement undetected—no small feat I might add since he was so stiff—Dave went upstairs to his room and doubled up on his clothing. He then came back down to the basement and shared once Mike got thawed out.

The really strange thing about this story is that not one of the adults ever noticed that Mike was wearing different clothes or ever found out that we had been to the river that day. I don't know why, but angels looked after three very disobedient children that day and loved us anyway. I'm so thankful that God's love isn't based on my goodness! I'm glad we can live and be forgiven.

> *"To the LORD our God belong mercy and forgiveness, though we have rebelled against Him" (Daniel 9:9).*

Figure 6: Spud checking out the glyn.

Chapter 6
"Spud" the Wonder Dog

Spud came into our lives in our later years and was a great wonder to us. First, because we wondered whatever possessed us to get another dog and second, because he was just so amazing. He was the grandchild we never had and consequently was spoiled rotten. Never had any previous dog been allowed on the furniture, much less the bed. It started out innocently enough. He was so little—then. By two years of age he had been in all forty-eight of the lower states because we couldn't bear to leave him behind when we traveled. Besides, who would want to keep him, seventy-five pounds of spoiled that he was? Never had any of our other dogs been allowed to beg at the dinner table. Spud practically had his own place setting. But then, as I said, he was amazing.

Rob and I took Spud to the vet soon after we got him for his first check-up. The vet said we'd better get a handle on this pup right away or he would take over our very existence. She said he was uncommonly bright and would certainly assume the role of pack leader if we didn't take matters in hand. Where was she when we picked out this puppy? Turns out she was right, and not a day went by but what Spud questioned if he couldn't handle things better if we'd just give him the chance.

We decided to take Spud to "Dog Obedience" class. This title is a trick to get people to enroll. Actually, it's people obedience and the dog just comes along to show if you've learned anything. It turned out that while I was somewhat slow, Spud was an eager learner. He was one of those students that was all eager with the "pick me, pick me" attitude; the "let me show you" student that always wants everyone to watch. So, things in class went along rather well as long as Spud was having fun. Practicing at home where there was no audience was an entirely different matter. I'd come into class complaining that I just couldn't get Spud to cooperate and the teacher would take him and put him through his paces. He'd perform perfectly with his head up and a smug look that silently shouted out that *he* certainly wasn't the problem here.

We were still working on "come" one fall day when Spud was still just a pup. We decided to scout out a lake for future canoeing. It was blustery and chilly, and the waves were choppy and the water cold. Rob thought we should let Spud off the leash. He was acting so excited about all that water that I wasn't sure he would come when he was called, but I was finally persuaded. The instant I let him go he plunged into the waves and headed out into the lake. I began to wonder if he was part lemming as he never hesitated, never turned, never responded in the least to our shouting and whistling. There weren't many boats out on the lake that day, but eventually one came by to see what all the fuss was about. By now we had gathered a curious crowd. The boat finally found him, still swimming more than a half-mile from shore. Well, I sure wasn't going to let him go near water again until we could work out that little problem.

> *We decided to take Spud to "Dog Obedience" class. This title is a trick to get people to enroll. Actually, it's people obedience and the dog just comes along to show if you've learned anything.*

By the next spring we had pretty well mastered the "come" thing, but I still wasn't sure he'd listen around water. My brother lives on a bayou that eventually finds its way into Lake Michigan. Rob and I took our canoe, a rope and a harness over to his place for the test. The idea was to wear Spud out, then work on coming. It was a beautiful, warm, sunshiny spring day. My brother decided to join us in his kayak. Spud was piloting the canoe without much aid from us and loving every minute of it. When we had gone about three-quarters of a mile and had started to get into marshy stuff, we decided to turn around. Spud would have none of it and with him out front it was either follow wherever he wanted to go or reel him in. I reeled him in next to the canoe and Rob finally got us turned around. Spud was still giving us fits about wanting to go the other way, so we decided to bring him aboard.

We were about a hundred yards offshore when we attempted this feat. Rob leaned one way for counterbalance while I pulled on Spud. First Spud got his front feet on the gunnels, then with a bit more effort, managed to get his back feet up there as well. So far, so good. Then, without any warning, Spud pushed off with his hind feet to clear the canoe and get back in the water. One second we were sitting in the canoe and the next we were submerged in the coldest water I have ever been in in my whole life.

Spud hadn't mentioned anything about the water being cold. In fact, he seemed to enjoy the whole experience. Rob and I on the other hand, couldn't even get our breath at first. My brother was totally useless as he was laughing too hard to be handy. Some folks working in their yard saw the whole affair and went running for their boats. When we were finally able to breathe and looked around to make sure everyone was accounted for, there was Spud sitting in the half-submerged canoe with a look that said—well, I'm not sure I should repeat it here.

At any rate, we were duly rescued and informed that we were surely the first swimmers of the season. My brother hadn't mentioned that the ice had been gone less than two weeks and when I asked him about it sometime later, he just shrugged and said he hadn't known we intended to go swimming. As for Spud, it would be a very, very long time until he would be invited to go boating again.

Spud has had brighter moments though. Our home was in a meadow that slopes away to a pond. I was working in the yard one day, spreading straw over a newly seeded area. I had brought the straw down from the barn in the tractor. I was hurrying because a storm was brewing. Suddenly, Spud started to growl. I had never heard him do that before and I was afraid that when I turned around, I might find some creature higher on the food chain than me. Spud was staring intently and growling and making me feel more uncomfortable by the moment. After a few tense moments, and realizing that so far nothing had grabbed me, I turned slowly around to see the tractor rolling slowly toward the pond. I must not have set the brake securely, and Spud had warned me in time to make explaining to my husband how the tractor had ended up in the pond unnecessary. What an incredible dog!

Another time, I was spacing the decking for our new front porch. It was about three to four feet above the ground and I was using the rather advanced technological method of two paint stirrers for spacing. It had been raining and was muddy. One of the paint stirrers slipped from my grasp and fell through onto the muddy ground below. Oh bother, now I was going to have to get underneath the porch and crawl around in that mess to get the silly thing. Spud had been watching and without a word from me, jumped down and retrieved the stick. Truly amazing!

We lived far off the beaten track—we even had to make our own electricity. One day when I was home alone with Spud, I saw him launch himself from the front porch in a frenzy of barking. I followed after to see what in the world was wrong, just in time to see two four-wheelers doing 180's in our driveway with Spud hot on their trail, barking all the way. Wow, this was amazing coming from my over-friendly, everyone who comes must be here to pet me, kind of dog. What a wonder!

Chapter 7
"Adventure Club"

My husband was working at a boarding school in Maryland and the boy's dean had his hands full. It seems there was an especially rowdy group of about ten boys the dean thought could benefit from some extra time away from the dorm. The dean asked my husband if he wouldn't be willing to sponsor an "Adventure Club." Rob, my husband, was plenty busy, but could tell the dean had just about had it with these guys, so he agreed to take on the project.

It was already October and the boys were anxious to get started. They wanted to do a canoe trip and because my husband didn't really have time to plan anything extra, he assigned the various boys' tasks. One boy would work with someone from town to plan a suitable route of not more than fifteen miles. A couple of other boys would acquire the canoes, paddles, flotation devices and something to haul all the stuff. Several boys would plan food for the day and make arrangements with the cafeteria and so on.

The date was set for a Sunday morning. The boy's dean agreed to pick up our van later that day and make sure it was parked, ready for us at our exit point. We could get six canoes, so Rob decided to make this a family outing. Our boys were two and three-and-a-half years old at the time and loved to go anywhere with their dad.

After the Saturday night activity, the "adventure boys" accosted my husband with the request to leave right away, thereby adding an overnight element to their adventure. Besides, they reasoned, we'd get an earlier start the next morning and we'd get back a little earlier on Sunday.

I guess it was the last point that won us over. We assured them we didn't have room for all kinds of camping gear and that, while our family could sleep in the van, they would have to tough it out on the ground with blankets. Of course, adventure seekers that they were, they loved the idea. Having anticipated this twist, they had gotten all the stuff ready and had it piled in the parking lot.

We loaded up and started off. We were young and _____. I'll give you the liberty to fill in the blank as the story unfolds. We had had nothing to do with the actual planning of this event, so were totally at the mercy of ten rowdy teenage boys.

The night was chill and damp, but we didn't have far to go. Even though it was late when we left, we were sure we could reach our destination well before midnight.

I don't know how familiar you are with the shape of canoes, but I can tell you from experience that if you don't have a proper canoe trailer, they are troublesome little things to stack. The boys had acquired a regular, flat car-hauling trailer with no sides and no center section. No matter how we tied those six canoes and no matter how slowly we drove, we would have to stop about every hundred yards or so to retie them. It was about 3:30 a.m. before we found the spot where we were supposed to put in. By then it was no longer chill and damp but downright cold with fog so thick it wasn't until daylight that we became aware of how close we had come to driving right into the river. The boys had tried crawling under the van to keep from getting soaked but had all ended up sitting in the van until first light. No one had slept, so we figured we might as well fix some breakfast and get going.

That's when we learned we were not traveling with natural-born cooks. The ones in charge of getting the food had gotten exactly what they had asked for—some pancake mix and syrup—nothing to mix it in or with, nothing to cook with, not even anything to eat it with if they could have cooked it. We perused the remainder of the grub. Instead of a crate and a half of drink, they had only picked up the half crate. We had enough sandwiches for lunch but nothing to go with them. We had planned to be back for supper, so we might as well get started. Cold, damp and hungry as we were, we had no idea that this was to be our bright spot in the day.

Our first challenge was getting into the canoes. The banks of the river were steep and muddy. We got the canoes into the river all right, but one after another as the boys tried to get down the bank they would slip and end up in the river. Ah, just part of a great adventure! When we finally got everyone settled into a canoe and headed downstream, we discovered that we had quite a variety of paddling skills on hand. They ranged from non-existent to fair to middlin'. We gave a quick crash course in the fine art of paddling and hoped things would improve as the day wore on.

We had paddled about an hour when Rob came to the realization that he had the van keys in his pocket. We were supposed to leave them in the van for the dean. We had come too far to try to go back but how would we get home with no van or trailer for the canoes? Things were not looking so great.

The river flowed an average of about four to six mph. At that rate we would reach our destination before lunch. As the troops began to fade, both from fatigue and famine, we urged them on with the promise of a fast food stop on the way back to school. By mid-morning, even those of us who had managed to stay dry were cold, so we decided to stop and build a fire. While that was a great idea, everything was so damp that about the best we could manage was your basic smudge and smoke affair. After about twenty minutes, we decided to give up on the fire idea and opt for some vigorous paddling.

There hadn't been anything along the river except woods and an occasional field. In the early afternoon we came to a place where the river widened out and slowed down. Way off to the left we could see some cabins. Ah, where there are cabins there must be people and where there are people there must be food. We were pretty sure it must be about lunch time because we could hear the dinner bell ringing. It appeared these people had no intention of sharing anything with us, however, because they were standing along the distant shore flailing their arms about and shouting obscenities at us. Obviously, these were not nice people. We headed to the opposite shore as quickly as we could. "Dam, dam, dam," they kept shouting while ringing their bell. All of a sudden, we became aware of the sound of falling water and realized these people weren't swearing at us, they were trying to warn us. Paddling even harder now, we barely made it to the shoreline before being swept over the dam. Whew! This was turning out to be more adventure than any of us had bargained for.

We portaged the canoes and all our gear around the dam and continued downstream. Our muscles had gotten sore, but with no other options except to keep paddling, the soreness began to work back out. We decided to put the best paddlers out front with the admonition to never lose sight of the canoe behind them. The next best paddlers we put in the back and we took the middle. Each canoe was to have one or more canoes in sight at all times. That worked rather well until someone in the second canoe needed a bathroom break. By the time we got started again, the lead canoe was nowhere in sight.

We all dug in with our paddles with the hope they would soon notice they were all alone and pull out so we could catch up. We paddled and paddled and just when our worry level was about to overflow, we came to a broad bend in the river. Over to the right were some rocky outcroppings and perched on top of one of them was one of our lost paddlers. About twelve to fifteen feet below him was the canoe with the other boy sitting in the bow holding onto some brush. I called to the boy on the outcropping to hurry down as we had a few sandwiches left and we were passing them out to eat as we paddled.

Who would have ever imagined? Instead of climbing down the way he had gone up, he simply hurled himself through the air with the intent of landing in the stern of the canoe. Much to the chagrin of the bow occupant, he was a pretty good aim. When he hit the canoe, the boy in the bow was catapulted high into the air, over the canoe and landed with a huge splash in the river. It was just like in the cartoons! We finally recovered from our laughter enough to help him back into the canoe and since there was no major damage, we were once again on our way.

> *Instead of climbing down the way he had gone up, he simply hurled himself through the air with the intent of landing in the stern of the canoe. Much to the chagrin of the bow occupant, he was a pretty good aim. When he hit the canoe, the boy in the bow was catapulted high into the air, over the canoe and landed with a huge splash in the river. It was just like in the cartoons!*

It was now late afternoon and still nothing looked familiar. The little boys had taken a nap but now were awake and getting cranky from hunger. The river was speeding up and beginning to take on a more ominous look. I wanted to take the little boys and walk out with them to the nearest civilization we could find, but no one else thought that was a good idea.

Suddenly we came to a very sharp, narrow hairpin curve in the river where a huge tree had fallen across almost the entire river. The first canoe found a chute on the far-left side but wasn't paddling fast enough to make it. They dumped over. The second canoe learned from their mistake and barely managed to remain upright. We were next and while we went for the same spot as the second canoe, our extra weight caused us to catch on a submerged branch and over we went.

As we surfaced near the canoe, we saw one of our little boys floating downriver where some of the boys from the first canoes were wading in the shallower water catching the varied flotsam from our canoe—including our youngest son. Our oldest son was nowhere to be found. I was terrified and praying fervently while we held the canoe and the other boys dove down to see if he had been pinned against the tree by the current. When they surfaced without him, we decided to turn the canoe upright and let it float on downstream to the first boys so we could all search. As the canoe was turned upright, there sat our oldest son clutching the gunnels with all his might. He had been there the whole time, upside down, holding his breath. With a prayer of thankfulness, we made our way to a sandbar to reconnoiter.

Everyone was wet now and still the end was not in sight. All the big guys pitched in. Some stripped the little guys, some tended to all the wet stuff, some rubbed the little guys with cloths until they were all pink and warm and some helped repack. Every one of the big guys offered something to wrap the little boys in so that, even without coats (now hopelessly waterlogged), the little guys could be warm. That meant all the big guys would be colder than ever. None of them would take back any of their offerings, so we loaded up and headed out again.

By now I was a basket case and every time I heard the river picking up speed it was all I could do to keep from crying. The chatter had stopped and we were all intent on paddling as fast as we could as darkness began to settle in around us. One more time we had a major crisis, but I jumped into the water to hold the canoe from turning and dumping over again. It was about 9:30 p.m. when we finally saw the lights of the house where we were supposed to get out of the river. We sent a couple of guys up to the house to call the school.

As we pulled up onshore and began to unload, one of the guys called out that he had found the van. We all ran over there to see how that could be. It had been hot-wired. Hmmm, the dean was more talented than any of us knew. About that time the folks from the house came driving down with blankets for everyone. They insisted we all come to the house for hot chocolate and sandwiches. Boy, they sure didn't have to ask twice.

Our conversation centered around what in the world ever possessed us to go out on that river—especially with those little boys. Didn't any of us know that that river had holes that no one knew where they went? They had lost cattle in that river. They and a neighbor had put a telephone pole down one of those holes and no one had ever seen it again.

So, before you fill in that blank, know that we learned the Lord takes care of those who haven't the sense to take care of themselves and that our preferred word would be "blessed." Our fifteen-mile trip turned out to be more like fifty or sixty miles. And finally, we took ten boys out, but we brought back ten men. They never asked for another outing. They were too busy helping with projects at school. And the dean never had trouble from that bunch again!

Chapter 8
The Big Bike Trip

Before moving from Maryland, we had discovered a wonderful historic trail that runs from Cumberland, Maryland, to Washington, D.C. The 184 ½ mile long canal was built to transport goods from the inland valleys out to the coastal areas. The towpath of the Chesapeake and Ohio Canal has been mostly restored and is maintained by the National Park Service. We had determined that riding our bikes the length of this trail would make a great family adventure.

The boys were five-and-a-half and newly-turned seven years old that summer. We rigged their twenty-inch wheel bikes with a banana seat, a tall bar in the back and tall front handlebars. We fastened their sleeping bag on the tall seat bar and a soft pack containing their clothing onto the handlebars. We rode twenty-eight-inch Raleigh three speeds with baskets on the front and packs on the back and carried a backpack as well.

First, let me say here that being frugal and maintaining good health do not always go hand in hand. The backpack was supposed to get us geared up for later hiking adventures—the ol' two birds with one stone thing. We obviously didn't have any distance riding experience or we would have known the two most vulnerable anatomical parts for bikers are the knees and the sitter. A full pack wears the knees in a way that I don't understand, but it is fairly obvious that the added weight of the pack ends up being absorbed by one's sitter.

Chapter 8 The Big Bike Trip   49

We took my husband's old cornet packed between two small pillows on top of his bike's front basket. All in all, we looked like gypsies running away from the caravan, but we at least had all the essentials. Well, almost that is. It seems we hadn't been able to locate any trail maps (not a problem nowadays with the Internet) or other information—minor things like campsite locations, availability of water and stuff like that.

We rolled into the town of Cumberland late in the day and found most everything closed. We had hoped to get more information on the canal once we got to town, but not only were most things closed, but no one we talked to on the street seemed to know anything about even where to find the canal. We finally learned about a general merchandise store that was open and drove there with the hope of getting some information. None of the clerks had ever heard of the C&O Canal but the manager not only had heard of it, but knew how to find it.

"Go out behind the store and although it is quite overgrown back there, you can get through it. You will come to railroad tracks. Cross those and go down a ravine and up on the other side will be another set of tracks. Follow the tracks and before long, you will find you are on a trail. That's it!" he said.

He went on to explain that the original place where the canal began had been covered over and partially developed. While there didn't seem to be an official beginning, we would find mile markers once we were actually on the trail. Today, you will find a park there and most everyone in town knows about it. They must have misplaced part of the towpath over the years because when we rode on it, it was 187 miles long and today it is only 184 ½ miles long.

We made arrangements to leave our car parked in the store parking lot and were assured the local police would also be notified to keep an eye on it. We then unpacked our gear, loaded it onto the bikes and began to push our way through all the underbrush, up and over the tracks, down through the ravine, up the other side and follow the set of tracks we found there. Sure enough, just like the man said, we soon found ourselves on a for-real path.

We followed the trail until we came upon a ballpark with a tall fence around it. The gate was locked, but inside the fence we could see a drinking fountain. My husband scaled the fence and filled all our water bottles just as dusk was settling in. We continued down the path, not knowing what was ahead or where we would spend the night. We hadn't peddled far when we found our first campsite. What a wonderful surprise! There was a large grassy area where we could pitch the tents, a hand pump for water, a porta-potty, a fire pit and even wood for the fire. Wow! After such a tenuous start this was turning out great!

The next morning, after we had made some breakfast and were packing up, a ranger came by and stopped to chat with us. He answered all our questions and gave us a map of the entire C&O Canal Towpath. Now we could know how far it would be to the next campsite, where all the locks were, where roads crossed the towpath and it gave us access to towns, any points of interest and a host of historical information. This was more like what we had in mind!

The kids were doing great on their bikes and we only had to cover about thirty miles a day. That meant we could stop along the way to rest or explore. Did I say the kids were doing great? Perhaps I should mention here that their dad was starting to calculate how far it was back to the car. He kept complaining that his knees were bothering him and he wasn't sure he would be able to do the whole trip.

"Ah, c'mon," I said, "the kids are doing great and I'm sure the aches will work themselves out." As the day wore on, we stopped more and more often—for dad. After rechecking his bike for any adjustments, I finally said, "Well, let me take the backpack for a while and see if that helps." Right away his knees stopped hurting and mine started. Not only the knees, but the bike seat seemed suddenly determined to gain altitude by pushing its way up through my body.

That evening, when we set up camp, I told the family that tonight we would have a special feast to celebrate our first successful day on the trail and proceeded to empty the backpack of all the canned goods we had brought. I wasn't entirely sure what we'd eat in the days to come, but I was sure that all that weight, minus the cans, divided up between four stomachs would be a lot easier to deal with than that overloaded pack. While we waddled a bit for the next day or so, we had no more knee trouble.

Each evening as we sat around our campfire, my husband would take out his cornet and practice awhile then serenade us with songs and hymns. The river was usually within sight and the notes would echo off the surrounding mountains. Ah, it was the stuff poems are written about. One evening, a group of Boy Scouts camped about a hundred yards down the trail from us. When my husband began practicing, it wasn't long before an envoy of Scouts came carrying a watermelon. (I don't want to even think about who had carried that thing all that way.) They came to barter some of their watermelon for an authentic rendition of "Taps" that night and "Reveille" the next morning. Definitely a done deal!

Chapter 8 The Big Bike Trip   51

Another evening, an older guy shared a campsite with us. An interesting fellow, he was living on the trail and continued going up and down all summer. As long as he didn't stay in any one place more than three nights, the rangers left him be. He was riding an old rattletrap bike and slept on the ground with one blanket and a piece of plastic. He carried everything else in one small daypack. Sometime in the middle of the night, we were awakened by a loud screech followed by lots of yelling. By the time my husband had pulled on his clothes and found the flashlight, the yelling had stopped and it seemed everything had settled back down. He decided to go out and have a look around. When he shined the flashlight down on the zipper of the tent door, there were two bright, little beady eyes staring back at him from the other side. A skunk family was checking out our campsite and it seemed better to just let them go ahead and look around than try to debate the issue with them. The next morning, the older guy came by to say goodbye and told us that he kept his oatmeal in his daypack and also used the pack for his pillow. He said he was sorry if he woke us, but that he'd been sound asleep when a skunk had tried to steal his pack from under his head and scared him half to death. He told us to skip the next campsite as there were marauding raccoons just waiting for unsuspecting campers there. We took his word for it and went on our way.

> *Sometime in the middle of the night, we were awakened by a loud screech followed by lots of yelling.*

We often stopped to take a short hike or go into a town if it wasn't too far. In town we'd stock up on fresh food, do laundry, get an ice cream cone or just look around. There were many historic sites along the way, especially as we got closer to D.C. On the Fourth of July, we took extra time getting ready since we hadn't seen anyone for a long time. We bathed in the river and put on our last set of clean clothes. Suddenly, we heard a bunch of yelling from around the bend upstream and across the river. Somebody was certainly in trouble. My husband took off running in the direction of the yelling and found two men in the river—one obviously trying to save the other and not having much success.

The opposite shoreline was lined with women and children shouting and screaming. The river here was mostly wide and shallow with a deeper channel near the middle. The younger man of the two had evidently lost his footing and was being swept downriver. My husband was a trained lifeguard and quickly swam toward the men while I stayed onshore with our two boys. He brought the drowning man over to our side of the river, since it was closer, and laid him down on a large, flat rock just out of the water. I bent down to see if he was breathing and was accosted by the very foul odor of stale beer. My husband was just in the process of starting to revive this guy when he regained consciousness. The guy looked at my husband and took a huge swing at him with his fist. Rob grabbed him and pushed him back under the water until he quit struggling, then brought him up for another revival. By this time the older of the two guys had managed to get across the river. He jumped on the younger guy's chest and sat there until that fellow finally settled down. It was a lesson on the evils of drinking that our boys never forgot.

We had set up camp for another night when two bikers came through and stopped to get some water. My husband went to talk with them and learned, among other things, that they were headed to Cumberland where they had no more idea how they were getting back to D.C. than we had of getting back to Cumberland. They soon rode off to do a couple more hours of riding before nightfall and my husband came back to our campsite. When he told me of the arrangement he had made with these two total strangers, I wanted to run and stop them. The keys to our first new car in a very long time were headed up the trail in the pocket of one of those guys! I was pretty sure we'd never see them or our car ever again.

We really didn't have much time to worry over the car as the next day the trail came to an end and a sign directed us to a local highway through the mountains. Once we got out on the highway, it was very apparent that the steep and winding highway with a fair amount of local traffic was no place for two small boys on bicycles. We returned to the trail and the map and discovered that this had been an area where the canal boats were directed out onto a dammed-up portion of the river. They would simply load up their mules and pole their way downriver until the canal picked up again.

Since we were short on both boats and poles, our only other alternative was to hike a path along the river that had been made by backpackers. At first the path was wide and clear, and it seemed we had indeed chosen the best route. Soon, however, the trail was hardly discernable with its overhanging veil of poison ivy. Also, the trail made its way along the edge of a cliff that dropped off anywhere from twelve to thirty feet to the water below. Sometimes we would have to hand the bikes up or down over large boulders. We decided it was time to stop and give our boys a little instructional philosophy. Since they both knew how to swim and the bikes didn't, we told them to walk on the outside edge of the cliff as they pushed their bikes. If they tripped or began to fall, they should push their bikes toward the mountain and we would be sure to rescue them if they fell into the river. The water was deep enough that we would not be able to rescue their bikes if they fell in and it would be a very long walk to D.C. if that happened.

It was very hot, there was no shade and we were being broiled in our own juices as the sun reflected off the rocks. Our oldest was behind me and evidently tired of keeping his bike always on the same side. Neither my husband nor I noticed when the boy and bike changed positions, but it wasn't long until we heard a blood-curdling scream and saw both he and his bike disappear over the edge of the cliff.

Running to where we had last seen him and could still hear him, we looked over the edge and saw his bike caught in a bush that was clinging to the side of the cliff. Farther down, dangling by one foot from another bush, was our boy with his head not more than a foot from the water. It took some time and soothing to set things right again, but aside from some minor cuts and scratches that we soon repaired, we were able to be on our way again. Both boys were now very willing to inculcate parental philosophy.

We had some friends visiting the D.C. area that had given us their local phone number and told us to be sure and call them when we got close to D.C. They would come out to the trail to visit with us. They had two children, a girl just a bit older than our oldest and a boy just a bit younger than our youngest. We called them from a country store we found not far from the trail. The people at the store advised us not to camp any closer to D.C. as there had been incidents of crime recently. We decided the 150 miles we had ridden thus far was probably enough at that rate and our friends volunteered to pick us up on the trail and help us find the guys that had our car.

Since our friends didn't have bike racks on their car, we decided to unload the packs into their car and the dads and the two youngest of our tribe would go in search of our car. The two oldest kids and we moms would ride on to the next point where a road crossed the towpath and wait there for the guys to come back with our car and the bike racks. The guys had phone numbers to call for the car and we figured it wouldn't take them much longer to return with our car than it would for us to ride on to our exit point.

My friend hadn't ridden a bike in many long years and was apprehensive about the whole idea, but I assured her that the miles would go quickly since we would be riding on level ground. Besides, we could stop any time she tired and wanted to walk for a while. I told her to watch for mile markers. We passed four of them before she noticed the first one. She couldn't believe she had ridden that far!

We arrived at the park before the guys and just lounged around in the cool grass while the kids threw rocks in the river. Before long we noticed that clouds were building up over the mountains and soon the thunder began to roll. Clearly, we were in for a soaking if the guys didn't arrive soon.

My friend began reciting all the horror stories she had ever heard about people being struck by lightning as the storm drew ever closer. The little park where we were to meet the guys was at the end of a dirt road with no houses or people anywhere near. About that time, a truck with one man in it drove in and came over to where we were. The first thing he asked was if we were alone. We assured him that we were waiting for our husbands whom we expected at any moment. He seemed much too curious for our comfort and we were greatly relieved when he finally left. It did take my friend's mind off the lightning, but I'm not sure serial killers were a positive replacement topic.

> *With the impending storm sounding ever more frightful, we decided to ride our bikes along the dirt road until we either met the guys, found shelter or the road forked.*

With the impending storm sounding ever more frightful, we decided to ride our bikes along the dirt road until we either met the guys, found shelter or the road forked. According to the thunder crashes, the storm was getting very close. We rode under a train trestle that offered only scant shelter. Since we weren't all that sure what would happen if we were under the tracks and the tracks were struck by lightning, we continued on. We crossed a stream on what could only be imagined to be a bridge; a few boards this way and that with gaping holes that showed the rocky stream about eight or ten feet below. We still hadn't seen any houses and the road forked not far ahead. We had just stopped to discuss if we should go back to the train trestle when we saw the same truck we had seen at the park returning. We were really spooked, but there was nowhere to run and nowhere to hide, so we just stood there fervently sending prayers heavenward.

Sure enough, the guy stopped and said he had come back for us because we had no business being out there in the storm, especially with these little kids. He wanted to load our bikes in the back of his truck and take us to shelter. He was very insistent, but we were firm in our refusal until lightning struck a tree about thirty yards around a bend in the road from where we were standing. Almost simultaneously I heard the now-familiar scream of my offspring. Not waiting to get on my bike, I bolted down the road toward the sounds of distress. I thought my eldest had decided to return to the imagined safety of the train trestle while we were debating with the man in the truck and that he may have been trying to cross the bridge when the lightning struck. It turned out he hadn't reached the bridge yet, but the resulting thunderclap certainly exhibited potential for stunting his growth. I found that he also had abandoned his bike and was running as fast toward me as I was to him.

This turn of events, accompanied by the now howling wind and continuous thunder, compelled us to toss the bikes into the back of the truck and scramble in after them. We left a canteen tied to a tree limb so the guys would at least have some idea where to look for our bodies. The man continued down the road a ways until we came to a very large, modern looking facility set back from the road and surrounded by high fencing topped with razor wire. He turned into this place and drove around to the back and into a large garage. Well, here we were locked into a building inside of a prison-type fence with a guy we didn't know. He told us to stay away from the windows and while my head told me it was because of the lightning, my heart was whispering other more sordid thoughts.

The facility was a completely computerized water treatment plant that piped its treated water out to the river. The man seemed very nice and gave us a tour of the facility after the storm died down. My imagination, however, was too busy creating some rather distressing scenarios as we stared down into the roiling vats of sewage for me to remember much of the technical details. Every fifteen minutes or so after the storm passed, I would ride my bike back down the now-muddy road to see if there were any new tire tracks. We really didn't know what to do except wait and try not to get hysterical. It had been hours since we were supposed to meet the guys and still there was no sign of them. It was already past twilight and heading for serious darkness when we finally saw headlights. I bolted for the road to intercept what surely must be our husbands. The dads were relieved to find us and quickly loaded our bikes onto the bike rack. We thanked the stranger for taking us in and said goodbye.

The guys had quite a story of their own. When they got to D.C. and called, no one answered at any of the numbers they had. It took them quite a while to track down someone who knew anything about these guys. The fellows that had our car keys had run into trouble on the trail and ended up walking all night, carrying their bikes. When our guys finally found them, they had blisters all over their feet and one had a sizable gash in his head from a tree branch he had encountered in the darkness of the night. All of this was because they had promised to be back in D.C. with our car by a certain time. So, instead of being disreputable, they were honest even to their own hurt. And finally, someone suggested much later that our adventure involving the man at the water treatment facility may have involved an angel since there was no need for anyone to be working there. Quite a sobering thought! Once again, proof that God takes care of His children—even the older ones.

Chapter 8 The Big Bike Trip 57

Figure 7: A big fellow just after finishing lunch in the pond.

Chapter 9
Horses, Horses

From my earliest recollection I have loved horses. It was my heart's desire, my fondest dream, my every wish to own one. My father always said I had had the misfortune of being born into the wrong family, but I was always hopeful that some birthday or Christmas morning I might wake up and find one standing outside our house by the curb. I read all the popular fiction stories about horses, I read books of facts about horses, I drew horses, I would even spend most of the day at the horse barn at the state fair hoping someone would discover they had one too many horses and would give the extra one to that kid standing over there—me.

One year, I went away to boarding school (my dad thought it was nicer to be able to tell the neighbors he sent his kid to boarding school than to reform school). At that school they had a horsemanship program and I was pretty sure this was as close to heaven as I was likely to get on this earth, or maybe ever according to my dad. At any rate, I learned about horses, I cared for horses and I rode horses. There must have been other kinds of activities besides horse stuff there, but it's hard for me to remember any.

In college I met a fellow that had grown up on a farm. I was under the erroneous assumption that the saying about not being able to take the farm out of the boy was actually true. He had even owned a horse. Why he would leave his horse to go to college was beyond reason from my perspective, but I married him anyway.

Chapter 9 Horses, Horses

He got a job teaching and one of his students that owned several horses invited us to go riding with them. I could hardly wait. The day finally arrived and we had a wonderful time except that I began to notice a particular discomfort as the day wore on. Before long, I was almost as anxious to get off that horse as I had been to get on it. It seems that while the saddle fit the horse just fine, it apparently didn't fit me.

When we got home, I asked my husband to check for me because I might need some first aid to parts I couldn't readily reach. He had me lay face down on the bed, and after checking the spot just above the tip of my tailbone, assured me that I did indeed need some first aid. We hadn't been married so long that I understood what that meant. In my family, merthiolate was considered a controlled substance for doctor's use only. We stuck to the very bland but colorful substance known as mercurochrome. It let everyone know you had been wounded without the torture of stinging and burning. The fact that you had to rinse the wound first was torture enough and the mercurochrome served mostly as your badge of courage. How was I to know my husband came from a family that valued grit above most other attributes and skipped merthiolate altogether and went straight for the alcohol?

I had never been interested in flying as heights made me woozy, but that day I mastered new height AND speed records. When my husband poured the alcohol on my worn-off sitting spot, I became instantly airborne. By the time I ceased circling the room, I was too exhausted to do any bodily harm to my husband. I must say that he would have been an easy mark curled up on the floor laughing his head off that way. He still laughs when I tell this story, but we're still married anyway.

I didn't have much opportunity for horseback riding for quite some time after that, but my desire to own a horse was as strong as ever. I was teaching my elementary students one day when the coach happened by and made a strange offer. "Anderson," he said, "I'll trade you a registered Quarter Horse mare for anything that doesn't eat."

Wow! A real horse! Right away I started racking my brain for something I could trade. We were currently renting a place on two acres near the university where my husband taught. We had been doing a lot of cleanup around the place and it was just possible we could make a place for a horse. It took us a few days to get all the electric fence up behind the house, but soon we were ready to receive my very first horse!

Her name was Baby, but I never quite figured out how she came by that label. She was broke to ride, but only with a bosal (a type of noseband used on a hackamore bridle) and had never had a bit in her mouth. She came from excellent cutting horse bloodlines and definitely had a take-charge attitude. Her previous owner recommended we break her to a bit right away, so we went shopping for a used saddle and bridle. It seemed a gentler snaffle bit would be a good place to start. She took it in her mouth without any fuss and as I adjusted everything, I made sure not to make it too tight. What I didn't know was basically anything! While the bridle setup was loose enough not to cause her any discomfort while standing there, it was also loose enough for her to play with the snaffle, grab it in her teeth and even flop it under her tongue. It was in the latter position when I pulled back on the reins and she started bucking like crazy. My husband said I looked just like the guys at the rodeo. Well, trust me, I wasn't trying to stay on that horse even for eight seconds. I just wanted to get off as quickly and with the least bodily damage as possible. So, lesson one, make sure the equipment is adjusted right.

> *My husband said I looked just like the guys at the rodeo. Well, trust me, I wasn't trying to stay on that horse even for eight seconds.*

The saddle we bought seemed to fit the horse OK, but the saddle horn was a hazard when she started her shenanigans ... which she did from time to time. I was starting to think horses looked best when admired from the ground. My husband tried to encourage me by threatening to get rid of the horse if I wasn't going to ride her. I told him he should ride her a bit himself. That way I'd have time to work on my courage as well as pick up some riding tips from watching. I'm pretty sure this horse suffered from equine PMS. At any rate, the second my husband swung his leg over her, she was off and doing her rodeo thing. She was showing real talent between bucks, stiff-legged jumps and twists when my husband went flying through the air. I'm not sure if he made eight seconds or not. I was, at any rate, very impressed. "Wow!" I said, "Did I look like that when I was on her?"

Since nothing more than his dignity was hurt, he simply brushed himself off and went to the house to call a horse trainer. It turns out the horse was not only talented but very smart—probably too smart for me. The trainer loved her and she performed impeccably for him.

We decided to fence the front of our property so Baby would have more pasture. Interpretation: less weekly mowing for us. We finished at just about dark and didn't think it would be a good idea to turn her out then. The next morning, I got up early and led Baby around her newly fenced and electrified pasture, making sure she noted her boundaries. The new fence made a corner near our bedroom window and I took her over there to ask my husband through the open window if he thought it would be all right to turn her loose. I wasn't paying that much attention and stepped in front of Baby to call to my husband. Baby backed up—right into the electric fence. I'm not sure of the exact sequence of the next events, but it felt a lot like she ran up one side of my body and down the other. I just held on—I'm not sure why—as she did a 180 on the various parts of my flailing body and took off at a dead run across the pasture. Somewhere midway across the pasture it occurred to me to let go of her rope, and to this day I'm quite sure one of my arms is longer than the other.

Whenever Baby came into season, which seemed like about every two weeks, she became very cantankerous and hard to manage. One day, we came home to find the pasture empty. The gate was latched and the pasture fence hadn't been cut or torn down. We couldn't understand how she could have disappeared or where she might have gone. We finally located a place along the back fence where hoof prints showed where she had landed on the other side of the fence. Not only was she a very talented bucking horse, but it appeared she might have the makings of a jumper—at least if she only had to perform when she was in heat! We were headed down the driveway to look for her when a stranger drove up. He wanted to know if we had lost a horse. It turns out she had smelled his horses miles away and went in search of some equine company. He had come home to find her tearing up and down outside his fences and she had his horses so riled up they were about ready to break through. He had tried to catch her but finally had to resort to roping her. He said she was in a stall in his barn, but he'd be grateful if we'd come get her as soon as possible because it sounded like his barn might not last much longer.

We were glad to get her back and it was about two weeks later that the same fellow drove up to our house. He wanted to trade a young filly that had identical markings to Baby's. He had taken it in for payment of a debt. He said he'd trade for anything that didn't eat. Hmmmm.

We traded a chainsaw that my husband hated using—he said the horse couldn't be worse than the chainsaw and promptly named her Chainsaw. I fussed and fussed about the name, but it stuck. Fortunately, while she looked like Baby, her temperament was quite the opposite, unless of course she just hadn't come "of age" and the whole PMS thing just hadn't kicked in yet.

I was still looking to purchase a different saddle when a group of riders came up our driveway one day. They had noticed our horses and wanted to know if we'd like to go riding with them. I explained the whole saddle thing and one of the riders said I should ride her horse to see if I liked that kind of saddle. I was finally persuaded to ride down the driveway and back and I'm sure half the county could hear me when I told my husband, "WOW! I don't need a new saddle; I need a new horse!"

> *I was finally persuaded to ride down the driveway and back and I'm sure half the county could hear me when I told my husband, "WOW! I don't need a new saddle; I need a new horse!"*

So began my love affair with Tennessee Walking Horses! The folks we had just met assured us they would help us find a suitable saddle AND an affordable Tennessee Walking Horse. Not long after they told us about a seven-year-old TWH gelding that needed a good home and would be affordable. They would get someone to bring him to us since the people who owned him lived some distance away. The current owners weren't taking good care of him, but he had been sweet-tempered and a good riding horse when they bought him. When the horse was delivered a few weeks later, we were shocked by his appearance. You could count his every rib and his backbone stuck almost through his skin. His hipbones protruded and his legs and nose were all skinned up. I certainly didn't want a horse that looked like that, but since the delivery person wasn't going back that way, and we didn't have the heart to send him back to such horrible conditions as he must have come from, we kept him.

At first, Razzle, as he had been named, wouldn't come near me, even when I held a bucket of grain. If he was afraid of me, he was terrified of my husband. Clearly, some man had made his life miserable. We kept him in a small paddock separate from Baby and Chainsaw and patiently worked with him until he began to trust us both. Gradually, he began to put on weight and filled out to a gorgeous, shiny-coated sorrel of about 15.3 hands. We decided that we'd sell Baby and Chainsaw to our horse trainer since he wanted them both and we'd start looking for another TWH. We finally found Spatz, a three-year-old bay TWH gelding with four white leggings.

Spatz was untrained and my husband undertook his schooling. We had a round pen and were making great progress with both horses. Our new friends helped us and it wasn't long before we could go riding with them.

I could look out my kitchen window to the pasture and see the watering trough. One day, I looked out to see Razzle with the garden hose between his teeth. He was pulling it all around the pasture. The faucet wasn't even in the pasture and I couldn't figure out how he had gotten it loose. As soon as I walked out of the house to check, he dropped the hose, walked over to the water trough and stuck his head down in it. It was bone dry! It seems one of our boys wanted to wash their car and had unhooked the hose in the middle, leaving part of the hose still in the horse trough. They hadn't hooked it back up when they were finished and with the hose end still in the trough, it had siphoned dry. Razzle was used to better service than that and was communicating his distress at not having his trough full. He never ran out of water after that and he never played with the hose again.

Another day, after roofers had finished putting a new roof on our house, my husband noticed Spatz standing out by the trough with one foot in the water. He would paw and paw and then stand there for a few minutes and start pawing again. We went out to see what on earth was going on. Spatz just stood there with one foot in the water until my husband backed him up. Since there was nothing in the water, my husband checked Spatz's foot and sure enough there was a roofing nail embedded in his hoof. It didn't take us long to remove it and doctor him and he never played in the water like that again.

Still another day, I was experiencing some distress related to living in a free-flowing testosterone

> *Winston Churchill once said that the outside of a horse was good for the inside of a man and I'm pretty sure that goes for us gals as well.*

environment and had gone out behind the barn to feel sorry for myself and shed a few tears in private. Razzle came over and stood close. Then he started to nuzzle me until I found I couldn't laugh and cry at the same time. He stayed there until I had regained my composure and then went off somehow knowing that I was OK.

Winston Churchill once said that the outside of a horse was good for the inside of a man and I'm pretty sure that goes for us gals as well.

Chapter 10
Practice Kids

There doesn't seem to be any really practical classes you can take to learn how to raise children. I suppose it has something to do with the fact that no two kids are alike, but my husband and I did have the opportunity to practice on someone else's kids before we had our own.

We hadn't been married quite a year when we received a phone call from my grandmother informing us that the family had gotten together and decided we should take my cousin, Skip, to raise. We were working at a Christian boarding academy at the time and he would enter grade nine in the fall. Well, plenty of people had pitched in on my own journey to adulthood, so we decided it was our turn to help someone else. We were young and idealistic. Fortunately for my cousin, he was young and resilient.

Skip's grandmother and my grandmother were sisters and handled his wardrobe. The only problem with that was they could never remember what they had sent him. If their local department store had a sale on underwear and he wore size twelve, they would buy him a dozen size twelve underwear, and since he was sure to grow they would also buy a dozen pair of sizes fourteen, sixteen and eighteen. Of course, the next time underwear was on sale, they would repeat this process, buying a dozen pair of sizes fourteen, sixteen, eighteen and twenty. This process was repeated with all of his clothing, although on a smaller scale. Needless to say, his underwear especially seemed to multiply like rabbits. Not wanting to seem ungrateful for all this bounty, he felt compelled to wear them all, sometimes changing three or four times a day. Shirts and pants worn for only an hour or two would be left on the floor or bed to be relegated to the laundry at some future time—either when I next entered his room or he found it hard to traverse his space.

Nothing I said with regard to this situation seemed to bring about reform and any words I spoke to the grandmothers about him not needing any more clothes fell on deaf ears. I wasn't sure which would give out first, me or the wash machine. I finally succumbed to force. If I found more than three changes of clothing laying out, Skip would get a licking. OK, then. A few days later, the inevitable happened. I came home from work to find the kid's room a mess. Seven! Count them, *seven* outfits lay strewn across his bed! By the time Skip came home, the hurricane-sized cloud around me had mostly dissipated to approximately the size of a summer thunderstorm but was still clearly recognizable as dangerous. He went straight to his room and stayed there for some time before coming out to face his own personal time of trouble. "I guess I'm going to get a licking, huh," he said. "Um hmm." "Well, I guess I deserve it. Who's going to give it to me?" "Rob will," I replied. Of course he would. I'd never even given the slightest thought to beating my own cousin. "When will he be home?" Skip asked. "Not until suppertime," I replied.

Skip went back to his room to do homework and I turned to the kitchen to work off my remaining adrenaline. About the time I had supper ready, the phone rang and Rob informed me that he wouldn't be home for supper as something had come up at school and he would have to be there rather late. "Oh no!" I exclaimed. "You have to come home; you have to give Skip a licking!" "Well, you'll just have to take care of it yourself," he replied.

Skip and I had a rather quiet supper and after dishes Skip inquired again about when Rob would be home. I assured him it probably wouldn't be much longer, and he returned to his room to finish his homework and clean up his room. After a while, Skip came out and asked me if I couldn't just go ahead and give him a licking since he had to get up early and really needed to go to bed. Whew! This kid-raising thing was a lot harder than I had imagined. I finally gave in and administered the first and last of a few weak, half-hearted licks that brought tears to my eyes and reform to Skip's heart. We settled on Skip learning to do his own laundry and I don't remember ever dealing with the laundry issue again. Well, I figured I'd better think twice before assigning punishment next time. Maybe the old "wait till your father gets home" approach wasn't all it was cracked up to be.

Another issue was the clock. Skip had learned to tell time a long time ago and even had a dependable watch. He actually did just fine unless he was fishing. Not being a fisherman myself, I didn't understand how fishing and time were incompatible. Skip didn't understand that coming home late brought all kinds of possibilities like drowning in the river, being chased up a tree by a bear, suffering life threatening injuries or being kidnapped by gypsies to our overactive imaginations. Eventually, we came up with an alternative to lickings—pushups!

Not long after we had initiated the pushup routine, Skip returned from a fishing adventure quite past his designated time. Rob added up all the minutes and calculated Skip's pushups. Seventy-five! He informed Skip that the debt needed to be settled before supper, so they went on the porch and Rob began counting. Skip had finished quite a few before he collapsed into a heap of sobbing, quivering flesh that vowed it was humanly impossible to do even one more pushup. Rob assured him that the debt must be paid and quietly got down beside him and finished the rest. There were more lessons learned that day than just about time! We tried to be creative in our instruction and I think we improved over time. Skip spent four years with us and he wasn't the only one that did a lot of growing.

Skip loved little kids. He started asking me embarrassing questions about why we didn't have any babies yet. I referred him to Rob. Rob told him that he wasn't having any babies until he had a movie camera so he could chronicle their lives. Since we didn't have money for a movie camera, he guessed we wouldn't be having any babies so that was the end of that. Or so he thought. Never underestimate the ingenuity of a kid! Sometime later, Skip came home all excited about a big secret! His boss was getting a new movie camera and had agreed to sell his old one to Skip. Then Skip could give the camera to Rob for Christmas and we could have babies! I was pretty sure I would just as soon have had the whole camera/baby thing be a secret! It was a really sweet gesture but I couldn't let Skip spend all his money just so we could have babies. Besides, I knew that if we got an older, used camera, Rob would never be able to get what he really wanted. I tried to explain all this to Skip but the disappointment on his face was hard to bear. It wasn't too many weeks until Skip came bouncing in one afternoon all excited—again. A teacher at school had overheard Skip talking to one of his friends about his disappointment regarding our "baby-less" condition and decided to help. (Great! Now everyone at school knew!) It seems the teacher had a relative that traveled to Japan and could purchase the prescribed camera at an affordable price. While his relative didn't normally provide this kind of service, the teacher was certain that for such a good cause, he could be persuaded. The short story is that Christmas that year was extra special and within an acceptable time we produced the expected offspring. Now we had two boys, Skip and Eric.

The following year, the boarding academy where my husband worked decided to close the dorms. Boarding seniors would be allowed to live with faculty or in approved village homes in order to graduate without having to transfer. We had a long discussion and determined that two boys were enough. We would not take on any other projects. Freddy, a boy that played in my husband's band, showed up on the doorstep one afternoon in early summer. I assured Freddy we would not be taking in any students the next year, but he was adamant. He said that since he was the only alto clarinet player and couldn't find anyplace else, we should reconsider. I told him he still had plenty of time to keep looking and since our decision had already been made, there wasn't much chance we'd change our minds. He said he'd come back later when my husband was home. I assured him he'd be wasting his time and put it out of my mind.

We were at the supper table one evening, just before school started, when there was a knock at the door. Upon opening the door, I was surprised to see not only Freddy and his luggage, but Freddy's parents as well. Some time and quite a few sideways glances later, Freddy was making his way up the stairs to begin the school year bunking with Skip. Now we had three boys, Skip, Eric and Freddy.

It wasn't long until we discovered two things. One was that having two high school boys, especially if one was a junior and the other a senior, would create an inordinate amount of competition in the household. The other was that Freddy was endowed with a very special talent: mainly that while he looked completely normal, he could fit incredibly extraordinary amounts of food in his mouth with no apparent harm or discomfort to himself. It wasn't long before these facts began to change our lives.

One of the first disasters we were able to thwart was the senior class officer elections. Always a secret affair until the senior class could concoct an amazing surprise, Skip had climbed on the roof of the principal's home next door and leaned out over the eaves to look through a window from whence he could observe the seniors meeting to elect their officers. Shortly, he came home looking like the cat that swallowed the canary. Recognizing the look, we began a quick interrogation that uncovered his plan to do his own junior rendition of the now not so surprising senior class election announcement. We were able to convince him that in the interest of peace and serenity for the entire next nine months, he might want to reconsider his coup. Besides, he hadn't attained his full growth spurt yet and we assured him that, while we loved him dearly, we would probably not be able to protect him from the entire senior class.

Sports was another area of contention. Our school had intramural teams that played a short season among themselves and then had a championship tournament. You would think that at least one time during the school year the boys might end up on the same team, but alas, that was not to be so. Furthermore, their competition always played out until the last moments of the season as their respective teams seemed to end up in the championship games. This guaranteed lively conversations at the supper table. Since this atmosphere did nothing favorable for digestion, we would try to derail the conversation and turn it to more positive subjects. More often than not, it would shift to Freddy's special talent and the bets would begin.

> *It wasn't long until we discovered two things. One was that having two high school boys, especially if one was a junior and the other a senior, would create an inordinate amount of competition in the household. The other was that Freddy was endowed with a very special talent: mainly that while he looked completely normal, he could fit incredibly extraordinary amounts of food in his mouth with no apparent harm or discomfort to himself. It wasn't long before these facts began to change our lives.*

Whatever the current weekly chores were, they would be offered as the object for betting. For instance, Skip would say to Freddy, "I bet you a week's worth of dishes you can't fit (this much of whatever we were having for supper) in your mouth." Freddy would then amaze us all by proving that he could. There would be follow-up banter regarding the particulars as in, "No fair, you didn't close your mouth completely" or "long enough" or whatever. Then the renegotiation process would begin as to whether Fred's performance was actually worth a whole week's worth of dishes or perhaps only a day or two. Needless to say, there always seemed to be a fair amount of tension between the boys.

We rented a home from the school. One day, I discovered by way of personal experience that a 220-volt electric heater in the bathroom had a short in it. While I had lived through the experience, I was sure no one would like to repeat it. I made sure the family knew to stay away from the heater until the school maintenance could come over to fix it. Skip came home first. He said he'd be careful but forgot that the backside of the heater was exposed on the stairs to the basement. A few minutes later, I heard a large object tumbling down the stairs. I ran to the steps and peered down in the basement and sure enough there was a moaning, groaning heap at the bottom that turned out to be Skip. He was slightly bruised from his tumble but otherwise uninjured. When Freddy came home a short time later, I made sure he was aware of the perilous heater and went back to the kitchen to fix supper.

> *Unsuspecting victims would be singled out to witness various bets about how much of any variety of food would fit into Freddy's mouth or perhaps something involving how much traffic Freddy could stop with his crippled person act or if he could get the bank teller to give him a quarter or…or…or. They never ran out of ideas!*

Shortly, I heard Skip's voice coming from the stairs, "I'll bet you a week's worth of dishes you can't touch that water pipe and that heater at the same time." "Don't touch that heater!" I yelled from the kitchen. But the prospect of a chore-free week was too much. Before I could get to the stairs, there was that awful rumbling, tumbling sound again. Sure enough, there lay Freddy, another moaning, groaning mass at the bottom of the stairs. As soon as he could collect himself the negotiations began: "OK, I touched it, so you owe me a week's worth of dishes." "Uh-uh! You didn't hold on to it long enough." "You never said…"

And they were off!

Perhaps of slightly less wonder, but still amazing, was Freddy's apparent total lack of shame or embarrassment. We would often take the boys to town as we were vegetarians and could not satiate their longing for hamburgers. We would drop them off in town with the reminder that if they ever wanted to return, they did not know us until the agreed meeting time and place. Off they would go. Unsuspecting victims would be singled out to witness various bets about how much of any variety of food would fit into Freddy's mouth or perhaps something involving how much traffic Freddy could stop with his crippled person act or if he could get the bank teller to give him a quarter or…or…or. They never ran out of ideas! We just knew that shopping would be a lot less embarrassing without them lurking in the background.

By the time Freddy graduated and Skip entered his senior year, we were expecting our second baby, another boy whom we named Scot. Skip was as devoted to the two babies as if they were his own. It was not uncommon to come home from a foray into town to find Skip sound asleep in the rocking chair with a sleeping baby in each arm.

Enter the inevitable girl/boy relationship morass. In the part of the country where we lived, it was not uncommon for girls to marry by the age of fourteen. Skip had a girlfriend whose parents suffered a bit of disappointment in that their daughter was already sixteen and not married. She lived not far from us and they would often invite Skip over to spend the afternoon. It wasn't long until we learned that the parents would find an excuse to go elsewhere, always assuring the kids that they would be alone for the rest of the time. Alarmed by the implications of this situation, we sat Skip down for a serious talk. Trying to reason with hormones is a hopeless job. Skip kept wailing, "You don't trust me!" Whew, this discussion was going nowhere. Silently I was pleading with God for something to say that would get through to Skip when I heard myself say, "OK, Skip, let me ask you a question. Are you normal?" "Of course, I'm normal!" Skip replied indignantly. "Well then, there you have it," I said, "Any normal teenage boy put in the situation of a girl inviting him into her bedroom with no parents on the horizon for hours is over-tempting his hormones. Fleeing is your only hope. If King David had paid more attention to Joseph's example, he could have saved himself a lot of grief. From now on, that needs to be your course of action." While it wasn't the most popular instruction we ever gave, it seemed to work. Skip went on to complete a very successful senior year and went off to college where he met and married his soul mate.

This whole experience helped us be much better prepared to deal with our own kids as they reached their teen years. I would highly recommend some "practice kids" to any young couple thinking about starting a family. To this day, we count Skip as our own kid even though we only had him with us for four years. Time marches on and his own kids have kids now. We have been so very blessed for having all of them in our lives!

Chapter 10 Practice Kids   71

Figure 8: Here's a fellow who knows a bit about camping!

Chapter 11
Camping 101

    I grew up in the city, but my heart belonged to the country. In fact, it not only belonged to the country, but probably to a whole other century. I longed for rivers and woods and all the wonders of nature as long as it didn't bite, stick or itch. I joined Girl Scouts to get away from the city, but all we did was have banquets and square dance. I took to the backyard with a blanket to throw in the hammock or throw over a rope to make a makeshift tent. Most of an afternoon could be absorbed getting the appropriate food, blankets, ropes, hatchets, matches and the rest of camping's trappings smuggled out of the house. Usually, a few friends and I would be about ready to settle in by sundown. What then followed was some semblance of the following scene: An adult, ranging anywhere from a parent, neighbor, aunt, uncle or grandparent would come out to see how we were doing. They'd pull up a lawn chair and begin telling us about the latest atrocity committed within a thousand miles. Just about the time dusk was getting serious and it was hard to see colors and details, they'd mention they had seen a stranger going down the street and they were pretty sure that same stranger was headed back our way. The adult would excuse themselves back to the safety of the house and leave us out in the dark to deal with the latest assassin, murderer, kidnapper or whatever was the highlight of their horror story. They sometimes would get to the house before we would, but not often. We became expert scoop and runners, but we never did master the overnight campout.

Life went on with one short interlude at a camp where we slept in tents. It was just under ten miles to the closest bathroom. I was the youngest camper and after the first day of listening to all the bear stories, I was pretty sure I was going to be in trouble that night. Sure enough, all that fresh air and water woke me in the night with an urgency that needed tending to soon. At home I had mastered the "whistle and run." It was my job to take out the garbage after supper and in the wintertime it was pitch dark by then. The theory was that if you kind of sauntered out to the garbage can while whistling, no bears would bother you, but once you took the lid off the can, you were fair game and had to run for your life back to the house. I was hoping that these country bears played by the same rules as the city bears. I whistled my way to the appropriate building then decided it was too far back to the tent and just stayed the rest of the night in a shower stall. I made note to bring my sleeping bag with me the next time. I was pretty embarrassed by my childish fears until I noticed the large number of sleeping bags airing out on tree limbs the next day.

Soon I was off to college where I met and married the love of my life—a farm boy no less—and I was sure he must be an experienced camper and that our future together would be full of all kinds of camping adventures. His first teaching job was at a boarding academy. It was tradition for the junior class to go on a camping trip in the late fall. You can imagine my excitement when we were invited to go along as sponsors. We had no tent or sleeping bags, but another sponsor rounded up some used equipment for us.

The first day was quite an adventure all in itself. It was a chilly October day and I was wearing a pair of bright red long johns my parents had given me the previous Christmas. During the rock-climbing phase of our day, my slacks caught on a branch that ripped out the side seam, exposing me to all manner of kidding about my long johns. Later, hiking down a canyon creek, I missed a rock that I was trying to jump to and got a good soaking for my trouble. Later still, around the campfire, one of my socks got too close to the fire and burned up before anyone noticed. By the time we were ready to turn in for the night, it had begun to sprinkle and I was having second thoughts about all this "river and woods" stuff. We were sleeping in a small pup tent that had a nice sewn-in floor. Our sleeping bags were two different styles and would not zip together, but we managed to finally reach the upper levels of hypothermia and fall asleep. In my dreams, I kept falling in the creek and getting soaked. I finally awoke enough to realize all was not entirely a dream. I *was* cold and wet, a condition that was getting worse by the moment. It was pouring down rain outside and it seems that while our cute little tent was entirely waterproof on the bottom, the top leaked like a sieve! We spent the rest of the night huddled atop a picnic table under a shelter with the one mostly dry sleeping bag serving as our only covering. Trust me, if one dry sleeping bag couldn't keep one person warm, then one partially wet one sure couldn't do the job for two people! It would be years before we would find the inspiration to sally forth into the great out of doors again.

We were teaching at another boarding school in another part of the country where my husband had a female student that took more than the usual interest in him. She lived at home and would often stop by the house just as he was getting home. I didn't feel particularly threatened by any of this, probably because it drove my husband crazy to have her around all the time. One Thursday afternoon the girl's parents called to see if she could stay with us for the weekend since they were having guests and would be crowded. We hadn't had any special plans for the weekend, but I knew this arrangement wouldn't be a good idea. I didn't want to hurt anyone's feelings and was trying to think of what to say when out popped, "Oh, we won't be home this weekend. We're going camping!" Great, that got us off the hook with them, but now we had to go camping and I had overlooked the fact that we still didn't own one single camping item. When my husband came home from work, I informed him we needed to go shopping for camping equipment. Even though we lived on an extremely tight budget, he managed to find enough money to buy some basics and get us started on the way to many delightful camping experiences! So, we had an over-attentive youngster to thank for many years of outdoor adventure including tent camping, backpacking, canoe camping, boat camping, motorcycle camping and even trailer camping (now my favorite).

One summer, my husband's parents had bought some land and asked us to come help them build a house. They lived about a hundred miles from the property and would only be able to help on weekends, but we could stay out at the place and get things started for them. We would live in tents, get our water from a bucket lowered thirty feet into a well, dig a latrine and use lanterns for light. Hey, if that didn't sound a lot like camping!

That summer we discovered that "real" camping wasn't for sissies. There's this thing about predators. Bears, mountain lions or wolves are one thing. They are at least big enough that you can see them coming and they at least have the decency to be large enough that you could actually hit them if you should need to shoot one. No, our predators didn't play fair at all. They were so small you couldn't see them coming. In fact, you couldn't even feel them crawling on you. Mosquitoes and black flies can be a terrible nuisance but they don't even begin to compare to the misery inflicted by ticks and chiggers! Each evening after a long day of scratching we would subject each other to a wide variety of torturous methods of killing each tiny little embedded chigger. Then we would pick the ticks off each other in much the same manner as chimps at the zoo. Our kids wore only bib overalls so the chiggers wouldn't have any help finding a place to call home. We didn't wear much more than that ourselves.

I had always heard about mountain men and trappers and other outdoorsmen not being welcomed in polite society because of the terrible odors emitting from their personages. That summer we had a firsthand history lesson. Those guys didn't smell bad because they didn't know anything about personal hygiene. They simply couldn't afford to have half their blood sucked out! We didn't have any bear grease handy, but modern technology had provided us with some equally smelly substitutes. Each morning we would each get a generous coating of mosquito dope followed by an equally generous layer of sulfur powder. Anything else that might be suggested was added to the mix. We even inquired into flea collars for kids.

Bathing was reserved mostly for rainy days. On wash days, we'd draw the water from the well and pour it into a small child's plastic wading pool and let the sun warm it up. The kids couldn't resist running through it and we didn't have the heart to tell them they couldn't since the days were hot. By late afternoon the wash water was slightly brown and full of grass but I would kneel down and scrub the few clothes we were still wearing and then draw fresh water for rinsing. This water was then used for family bathing as it was now dark enough not to frighten the casual passerby with nudity run amuck.

As it turned out, all this experience with the out of doors came in pretty handy when we retired to what most of our friends considered a very primitive lifestyle. While we didn't have electricity from town, we did make our own, had wood heat, and a deep well that worked most of the time. We would see the occasional black bear, mountain lion, wolves, and even a grizzly from time to time, but moose, elk, deer, geese, and turkey were regulars. We even had a militant grouse along our driveway that would control the traffic flow any time she took a notion. The important thing was that while we did see two ticks in thirteen years of tramping in the forests, we never encountered one single chigger!

So, my advice to you is to get outdoors! You have no idea where it might take you!

Figure 9: Moose twins learning to swim down at the pond.

Chapter 12
What's So Grand About that Canyon?

Our kids were getting older and Christmases were getting more expensive. Toys were a thing of the past and electronic equipment and trips were all the rage. My brother, who lived in Arizona, offered us a place to stay in Flagstaff if we wanted to come out there and ski over Christmas vacation. The boys thought that would be awesome, so we collected some friends and headed west.

The first day on the slopes seemed to be going well enough. The kids were having a great time and we three parents who had chosen to ski seemed to be having a great time as well. My husband is a half-day skier then packs it in while I like to stay out and get in a few more runs. The other dad wanted to stay out longer as well but was not comfortable following me as he had been skiing with Rob, my husband, all morning. I assured him we could stick with the same runs he had skied that morning and I would be happy to follow him. He finally decided he would do that, and we headed for the chair lift to the top. As we ascended the mountain, I suggested we might want to get off at midway since we might be a bit tired and the route down from there was less strenuous. Our friend assured me that he and Rob had always gone to the top and because he was familiar with that route he would continue to do so. OK then. Arriving at the top, I let him lead. Not far down I saw him disappear over a rise then saw a large poof of snow. Oooh oh, that couldn't be good. I hurried to the place I thought he should be and sure enough, there in a blob of snow lay the twisted form of our friend. Our conversation went something like this: "Are you OK?" *pause* "No." "Should I go get the ski patrol?" *pause* "Yes." "Shall I straighten you out a bit first?" *pause* "No, I think I'd like to just lie here and practice a little pain management." "OK then."

So, our friend spent the rest of his holiday in bed, barely able to care for his personal needs. Unfortunately, all of their money was in travelers checks in his name and he couldn't get out to cash any of them so we were hard pressed to come up with enough of the green stuff so the kids could go skiing the next day. We finally came up with a "plan" (see chapter 1 to see where this is headed) we thought would work for everyone. Rob and I would drop off the four teens at the ski slope and pay for their day of fun, leaving us with about $36 cash. We would then head for the Grand Canyon to hike to the bottom, something I had *always* wanted to do. Our friend would be at the motel in bed while his wife went sightseeing in Sedona until time to pick up the teens after skiing. Sounds harmless enough.

There are two main trails to the bottom of the Grand Canyon from the South Rim: the Bright Angel, and the slightly shorter Kaibab Trail. We thought that since we would be doing a down and back in one day trip, we should take the shorter, but steeper, Kaibab Trail. It was a beautiful, cool, sunshiny, winter day and while we didn't have proper hiking gear with us there were water sources at various stops along the way, or so we had been told. (I guess they shut things off for winter just like everyone else. What were we thinking?) Ah, it was one of those bucket list things and I was excited about the prospects of touching the water in the Colorado River.

We reached an overlook where we could see the river when my husband announced that he had gone far enough. He was quite content to stay right there while I continued to the bottom, touched the water, and came back up to meet him. I knew that would take hours and was quite sure by that time he would be back at the top snoozing in the van. I was trying to convince him to continue the adventure when a mule train from the bottom came into the overlook for a rest. The ranger in charge of the supply train came over to talk to us and after learning our situation suggested we spend the night at the bottom. He radioed down and discovered they had two bunks left in their respective dorms and we had just enough cash to cover the cost with enough left over for something to eat. WOW! This was way better than we had ever imagined! He assured us they had a pay phone we could use down there so off we went to explore the GRAND Canyon via the Kaibab Trail.

When we reached the camp and settled into our dorms we went in search of sustenance as we had only had a light breakfast. We were able to purchase an apple, an orange, a Snickers candy bar, and a turkey sandwich. (Being vegetarians, we contemplated throwing out the turkey and just eating the bread and butter but thought better of it since those few items had to get us out of the canyon the next day.) So, for supper that evening we split the orange and sandwich then shared the apple and candy bar the next day. Our next task was to make sure our family knew we were OK and that our plans had changed. It turns out that the phone was only usable with a special credit card which we did not have and the operator would not allow us to make a collect call or charge the call to our home phone without someone being there to verify the charge. We went round and round with her explaining our situation and that before long our kids were going to be calling for a very expensive search and rescue operation to begin that only she could thwart and that should she fail to do her part we would be sending the bill her way. She finally agreed to let the call go through and let our kids know we were spending the night at the bottom of the Grand Canyon. That evening we were able to touch the river and even hike part way up the north rim trail before turning in for the night.

We woke early the next morning to an historic event. It was snowing at the bottom of the Grand Canyon! That rarely happens. What we didn't know was what was happening those several thousand feet up at the south rim of the canyon. We were the first ones out of camp that morning as everyone else took the time for daylight and a substantial breakfast. Our breakfast was eaten on the trail—our half an apple and half a candy bar. We decided to hike up the longer, but less steep, Bright Angel Trail even though it meant we would be miles from our vehicle once we reached the rim. It was a wonderland in the half-light of dawn. Wildlife was everywhere, including some exceptionally large mountain sheep that seemed determined to own the trail. There wasn't really room for all of us on the narrow path and it took a good deal of arm waving and loud noise to convince the critters to go another way. Having gained the right of way to the trail again we continued one step at a time.

As our energy waned from both lack of food and water other hikers began to catch up with us. Some merciful souls shared their bounty for which their generosity was noted in heaven I am sure. A cup of water and about six to eight peanuts certainly made an extreme difference in MY day. I was able to finish the hike at something more than a snail's pace. The other phenomenon was that the closer we got to the rim, the heavier the snowfall became. By the time we reached the rim it was experiencing blizzard conditions, and everything was closing, including the roads. We searched in vain for a ride to our van but most of the services had already shut down. We finally found one fellow who was willing to take us to our van (for free) and help us dig it out of the snow. (I wonder, was he really a man?) The Lord certainly was taking care of us that day! As we headed back to Flagstaff, we listened on the radio to the highway announcements of road closures—each time the exit we had just passed! So, we made it safely through another adventure and now we have another conversation to look forward to with our guardian angel! And yes, we think the Grand Canyon is indeed *Grand*!

> *"My help comes from the LORD, Who made heaven and earth"*
> *(Psalm 121:2)*

Chapter 13

Motorcycles Aren't for Sissies

We had moved to Scottsdale, Arizona, and in those days the desert stretched for miles around us. At first the heat (who in the world moves to Arizona in July?) and all those rocks were depressing. The color of almost everything was a very uninspiring brown. What had we been thinking?

After our first summer we decided that, perhaps if we could get more up front and personal with the desert, we could learn to like it. We bought two Kawasaki 100 on/off road motorcycles. Our boys were preschoolers and were ecstatic with our acquisition. The day after the bikes were delivered, the four of us took off on our first foray into the desert. We rode, quite successfully I might add, for a time before we came to a tall dike. The trail went right up along the top and the riding was especially easy there. After a number of miles, the dike had a rough break in it but then continued on.

We had the boys get off and my husband went first. He successfully maneuvered the rock-strewn trail down and then up the thirty-foot embankment. It was my turn next and he told me to be sure and be in first gear when I got to the bottom as it was all the bike could do to get up the steep bank even with a running start. I was concentrating on all those big rocks and had been shifting down. When I reached the bottom, I gunned it only to realize in my inexperience that the bottom on the shift lever was neutral, not first gear. I put it in first gear and started up the other side from a dead standstill and made it all of three-quarters of the way up before the engine sputtered and died.

Once again, my inexperience kicked in and not knowing how to turn on the steep hillside, I started sliding backwards. I ended up tumbling with the bike sometimes ahead and sometimes behind until we both reached the bottom—me in a bruised and bleeding, sobbing puddle, my brand-new helmet with a gouge in the side and my sporty new bike scratched and with a broken mirror. I wasn't about to try that again, but my husband assured me that the boys were too young to drive and it was miles back home. I would just have to get back on and ride—once my husband drove it up the dike for me, that is.

> *I ended up tumbling with the bike sometimes ahead and sometimes behind until we both reached the bottom—me in a bruised and bleeding, sobbing puddle, my brand-new helmet with a gouge in the side and my sporty new bike scratched and with a broken mirror.*

He took my bike on down the canal until he found a place he could get a good run at it and get back on top of the dike. By then I had at least stopped sobbing, although it would be quite some time before I quit feeling sorry for myself. I stayed closer to home for a time after that, but ventured out to get the mail one day when a neighbor friend stopped me to ask if I knew how to do wheelies. Since I didn't, he took it upon himself to teach me, all the while assuring me that my husband would be so proud of my prowess.

I practiced for a while in the parking lot before returning home. When my husband came home, I hurried him out behind our house to the desert to show off my newly learned stunt. Of course, I wanted to impress him, so gave it even more gas than I had practiced. I started going over backwards, so I hit the brake to bring myself back down. That turned out to be too much as well. I was coming down with such force that I started to imagine how I might look in dentures. The only solution I could think of was to go back up. I didn't seem to be able to figure out how much was enough, so I proceeded across the field bobbing up and down like the bobber on a fishing line with a big catch. When I was finally able to get back down on two wheels, I was so relieved I didn't even notice the sarcasm in my husband's voice when he said, "Now, that was real special."

These two "near death" experiences were nothing compared to what awaited out on the streets and highways. I soon came to realize that only the very paranoid lived very long out there.

The school was going on a campout near Prescott, Arizona, ... literally *up* from Phoenix. We decided to ride our motorcycles. We loaded all our gear and kids on the back and started up the interstate. That's when we learned how friendly the family of bikers is. Everyone hollered and waved. Our poor little bikes huffed and puffed all the way up that long grade and it wasn't until much later that all we took to be friendly calls and gestures were more along the lines of, "Hey, look at those fools on those little bitty bikes with all that stuff trying to get up this mountain!"

We did make it, though, and even survived a tornado on the ride home. I also learned at a later time that if a front tire blows out at high speeds, it can be a wild ride. Next time, I'll know better what to do; meanwhile, I'm looking forward to some very interesting conversations with my guardian angel when the Lord comes.

We morphed through a number of ever-increasing cc's (the size of the engine on a motorcycle) over the years until we finally arrived at two Yamaha 650 Maxims. Ah, now we could do some serious road trips. The boys were in their early teens by now and not yet able to drive, but these bikes could handle all of us and, with a few modifications, our gear as well. By the time we got the bikes ready, we didn't have enough money left over for proper riding gear, but we figured with a little creative layering we could manage.

We left Phoenix on a beautiful, sunshiny day. We were headed up the mountain to Flagstaff to meet my brother, then strike out for Colorado via backroads. As we left Flagstaff, we encountered our first challenge, the wind. We were fortunate that it was steady because we had to lean our bikes so far that a sudden change would have dumped us right over. By the time we got to Colorado, we ran into snow and no matter how many layers we put on, we were slowly freezing. We decided to get down out of the mountains as quickly as possible but ran into rain that caused mudslides and closed roads. It continued to rain steadily at the lower altitudes and even duct tape and garbage bags couldn't keep us dry. By the time we stopped at a rest area, I needed help getting off my bike. The hand dryer in the rest room wouldn't work, so I ended up handing my clothing out to the guys to dry in their rest room.

We now have a special relationship with most all of the overpasses leading to Denver. We would stop, climb to the top to get out of the wind and huddle there until we quit shivering, then head for the next one where we would repeat the process.

We stopped just north of Denver to stay a few days with friends. I spent most of my time there in front of their fireplace where they kept a roaring fire. When I finally quit shivering and began to feel my appendages once more, they came up with this great idea to take us to visit Rocky Mountain National Park. Mountains! Yikes! There was no way I was getting near anything that looked like a mountain anytime soon—at least not on a bike. Two of their family members thought it would be fun to ride the motorcycles up there, which I thought was a great idea as it would assure me a place inside a warm vehicle. That is until we got back to the house and I discovered I now had to share the fireplace with two more people.

After we left Denver and started across Nebraska, the weather warmed up. Spring storms came late that year, so a couple of times we had to take detours because of predicted softball-size hail and tornadoes. Once we got to Lincoln, Nebraska, we left all the bad weather behind and the rest of our trip was clear sailing. Of course, you know, I'm only referring to weather here.

The purpose of this trip was to do a mini-roots thing for my husband (a genealogy study on a small scale). Little did we know that the whole of eastern Iowa considered him a perfect poster child for prospective parents. Ah, the boys and I listened to so many of his parents' friends expound on what a wonderful child Robert was, how they only hoped their own children turned out to be like him and on and on and on until we began to wonder. I guess he must have used up all that perfection as a child because while the boys and I love him dearly, we had seen a crack or two in that image over the years.

Our trip home was pleasant, but we gave up camping for hot showers, soft beds and swimming pools. We decided upon arriving home that we didn't want the boys out on the streets on motorcycles until they had acquired the proper amount of paranoia, so we sold them—the motorcycles, silly! All in all, we can assure you that, while motorcycles are lots of fun, they certainly aren't for sissies!

Figure 10: *Checking out the ladies.*

Chapter 14
Mexico or Bust

The date was 1967 bc (that is to say before children and not to be confused with BC). I was teaching third grade and my husband and I had one "practice kid." Another teacher and I would often meet after school to grade papers together and dream of the day when we would have children of our own. They, of course, would be perfect and would certainly not act the way some of our students did. My friend had had this dream for about seven years, but it was relatively new for me. Actually, the dream was soon to become a reality as I had just found out that Rob and I were expecting our first baby.

My husband, along with my friend's husband, decided we should spend Christmas in Puerto Vallarta, Mexico, that year and while neither family had the financial resources to accomplish such a feat, the guys assured us they could figure out the details. Our friends had friends in Mexico that could provide us a few days' stay in Guadalajara. These folks also had connections in Puerto Vallarta and could not only help us find suitable accommodations there, but also help us with the proper food and water adjustments that foreign countries require.

Ah, we were young and optimistic! We had a new Volvo bustle back and the guys figured we could leave Nashville, Tennessee, and drive the forty-odd hours straight through to Guadalajara. I must mention here that Skip, our "practice kid," was looking forward to spending the holidays with his Grandma and family in Michigan so he would not be joining us on our trip. School had closed early that year for the Christmas flu epidemic. My friend was sick and it didn't look like she would see anything white that Christmas except sheets. The day before we were to leave, the doctor finally released her, reminding her to get plenty of rest. We made it to Texas before we hit ice storms so severe we thought we might have to return home. We saw a car or two go twirling off the road, but we managed to drive through the storm. Once we got to Mexico where the roads were straight and only the horizon interfered with the view, our friend's husband would gleefully put the gas pedal to the floor while declaring that this indeed was what Volvo's were made for. About the only thing we saw for hours on end was an occasional cow or burro standing mournfully alongside the road waiting for us to get close enough so it could jump into the roadway.

We met and made new friends in Guadalajara and were able to spend a few days getting acquainted while resting up. They had an eight-month-old baby that we all found to be entertaining—at least until we got to Puerto Vallarta. Our motel there had four rooms—we rented three of them. They all had huge sliding doors and the ceilings opened to all the other rooms for circulation. We soon discovered that the baby was used to having a room to himself and wakened at every sound and movement made by his parents. The occupants of the fourth room turned out to be three single fellows come to town for the Christmas celebration. The baby had just finally settled down in the wee hours of our first morning when the three fellows came home. They tried to be quiet but the baby heard them anyway and started crying again. Much later, we were all lying there quietly hoping for the impossible when we heard a very frustrated male voice in broken English loudly proclaim, "Shutupa, you baby you!" They left early that morning before any of us were up, so the first order of the day was to hurry over to the manager's house and rent the extra room for the remainder of our stay. We agreed to split the cost of the extra room to provide the baby his accustomed seclusion.

> *About the only thing we saw for hours on end was an occasional cow or burro standing mournfully alongside the road waiting for us to get close enough so it could jump into the roadway.*

We went swimming one day at Mismaloya, a nearby abandoned town built as a movie set. We drifted out beyond the breakers, thoroughly enjoying ourselves until someone noted that the swells were getting awfully big. Since I was the furthest from shore, it took me the longest to get in and when I could finally stand up in the shallow water, I found myself caught in a riptide. I was being swept back out to sea and I couldn't even move my feet. I called for help and my husband came running to save me. Of course, he became trapped as well until a towering wave came in over our heads and knocked us both down. We were rolled over and over and washed up far enough that my husband was able to pull me to safety. He was scraped up and I broke a few toes.

The toes didn't really matter that much because within the next few days my entire intestinal track turned against me. It wasn't long before my moaning and groaning became a duet as my friend's husband succumbed to a similar fate. We had gone out to a village on the morning that I got sick to have a local fisherman take us out in his boat, but by the time I got there, I knew I wasn't up to it. I stayed in the car and soon relieved myself of everything I had ingested within what seemed the last several months. Misery was my only companion as I lay moaning in the car. The world seemed to have a faded existence and I felt oblivious to anything going on outside my body. After a bit, a persistent and strange snuffling sound coming from just outside the car raised me to a new level of awareness. I sat up to look and saw a number of large pigs rooting around. I was too sick to try and shoo them away but soon heard another noise. When I sat up again, I saw a very small boy wearing a very large pair of pants. He was yelling at the top of his lungs while holding the pants up with one hand and twirling his belt with the other to chase the pigs away. It should have been pretty funny to watch but I couldn't find even one giggle wedged between all those moans. So that was pretty much the end of vacation for me. My friend's husband joined me about a day later. One afternoon a couple of days later, I was lying awake in bed when the caretaker's young daughter came to replace our water bottles. She returned with the first one much faster than I would have thought possible as her home was some distance from the motel. When she left with the second bottle, I mustered up enough strength to follow her. She rounded the corner of the motel building and stopped at the outside spigot. I was dumbfounded to realize that she had stopped there to fill up our water bottles. No wonder we were sick! Those newly introduced microbes were finding strong objection in at least two of our systems.

From the account at the end of each day for the rest of the week, my husband and my friend had a grand time from horseback riding to sightseeing. My friend's husband and I were having a hard time finding enthusiasm for much of anything, but were glad that at least someone was having a good time. From then on, we would all joke about my friend's husband and I needing to take a trip back to Mexico and finish our vacation. Somehow though, Mexico had lost its charm for the two of us. Besides, I was pretty sure there was still plenty I hadn't seen of my own country yet.

Our return trip home took much longer as so many extra stops were required. We were so thankful of heart to still be alive and we had gained a much greater appreciation for clean water. No harm came to our baby and our friends counted the trip a success as they managed to come home pregnant with their first child! Don't ask me, I have no idea how they did that!

Chapter 15
"The" Boat

No one tells you until after you have purchased your first boat that you have just experienced one of the two happiest days of your life. The other happiest day will be when you sell it. At any rate, it doesn't really matter because at that point you're really not equipped to understand what they're talking about. This is the story of "The," the only real boat we ever owned.

Not many of us first-time boat owners have the financial backing to actually buy a new boat; so, for the purpose of this writing, you may assume we didn't either. We found our perfect solution ... a used, twenty-one foot inboard-outboard "party barge." It had enough horsepower to satisfy our teenage boys for skiing and enough room to walk, eat around a table and sun on the deck. The awning needed replacing and there was a big hunk missing from the backseat from time spent sitting in a pasture. It seems the resident horse there resented the intrusion.

Now, experienced boat owners will immediately recognize the problems that can come from "sitting." We, however, had not a clue and took our speedy sample run around a small nearby lake to mean that everything was shipshape.

Our first run was with some friends who were somewhat nervous about going out with us. I am, if nothing else, a good persuader and soon had them talked into a harmless spin around the lake. We got the boat launched without mishap and headed for the dock to pick up everyone.

Chapter 15 "The" Boat

We had barely cleared the launch area when one of our now more than somewhat nervous friends mentioned that they were pretty sure the boat was sinking. Before we had a chance to respond to the ridiculousness of the idea, several others began to mill around looking for life jackets and one high-pitched voice screeched that they didn't know how to swim. In the midst of the ensuing hysteria, we were forced to admit that the boat was indeed riding lower in the water and might even be sinking. We headed back to the launch posthaste and arrived just in time to put in the bilge plugs before the boat bottomed out. By the time we got the boat loaded on the trailer, pulled from the water and the water emptied from the bilge, our friends were nowhere to be found. Perhaps if I could have found them right away and convinced them to try one more time, things might have been different. From that time on, whenever we asked them out to the lake, they were always busy and never seemed to have time for fun anymore. Lesson number one: ALWAYS check to see the plugs are in place before putting the boat in water!

Since several families had been involved in our maiden mishap and they seemed eager to share their embarrassing overreaction to a mere near-drowning incident, it became increasingly difficult to find folks willing to share the sun and sand experience of boating in Central Texas. No problem. We had friends in other states. We'd invite them!

By this time, we had had a new awning made for the boat and replaced two small backseats with a raised deck suitable for sitting or sunning. By the time our friends from Arizona arrived, we were ready for bigger and "badder" lakes. The day dawned bright and clear, but by the time we got everyone ready and loaded up and drove the distance, it was almost lunch time. We headed out across the lake where we could find a secluded spot to enjoy the afternoon.

We spent the afternoon anchored in a lovely cove with time spent swimming, eating, visiting and lounging about. By late afternoon, a stiff breeze had kicked up. In Texas it's called a stiff breeze, in most other parts of the country it's called a gale. We decided to call it a day and headed back across the lake where our truck was parked. As soon as we left the protection of the cove, large waves began to break across the bow and onto the deck. It soon became apparent that the deck was not draining properly and that we were sitting lower and lower in the water. When our engine sputtered and died, we discovered that instead of draining out the sides, the water had been draining into the engine compartment. We set our awning to catch the "breeze" and were able, through a combination of wind and wave power, (not to mention all hands in the water trying to swim the beast to shore) to sink the boat fairly close to shore—the far shore from where the boat launch was. There were no houses on this side of the lake and only a few rutted trails leading to where—we had no idea.

We began to hike away from the lakeshore hoping to find someone that might take us to the other side of the lake. Just as it was getting dark, we came upon some campers who loaded us all up and transported us back to our truck. By the time we got home, it was very late and while our visitors assured us they were still our friends, there was no way they were interested in boating with us ever again, even if we could get our boat off the bottom of the lake.

It took quite a bit of time, help from some boat-owning friends and a considerable amount of money to reinstate "The" to boat status. (By this time our efforts to name our boat had died for lack of enthusiasm and because of its seemingly determined search for the bottom of the lake it simply became "The.") It seems the drain tubing had rotted over time and drained the water into the bilge instead of back out into the lake. Of course, the boat had to be practically dismantled in order to do the repairs and the damage to both the inboard and outboard engines from being submerged was significant.

By the time we got the boat back home, our new truck was showing itself unworthy of travel. The brakes pulled to the right with even light pressure and a panic stop could throw you into a full-on broadside slide. After numerous unsuccessful trips to the truck dealer for repairs, it was finally agreed that they would loan us a vehicle for our long-awaited family vacation to Lake Powell. I must explain here for the benefit of any readers who, like our dealership personnel had never heard of Lake Powell, that it is a very large lake in Arizona. Perhaps it was presumptuous of us to assume that everyone has heard of Lake Powell, but in our defense, they never asked either. Let's just say that they were less than happy with the number of miles we accrued on their "loaner." Well, back to the story.

We enjoyed a wonderful time in the lake. It is much too hot at Lake Powell in the summertime to spend life anywhere else. We considered ourselves experienced boaters by now and had hardly any trouble at all. At least, if you don't count the time we almost broke the boat in half from being slammed down on a very large wave created by an afternoon "breeze."

The time came for us to head back home to Texas. We were feeling pretty good about the whole adventure when suddenly one of the tires on the boat trailer went flat. We were in that wonderful nothingness of New Mexico in the middle of an Indian reservation and we had no spare. My

Chapter 15 "The" Boat   93

husband ended up spending the night alone on the boat while the kids and I headed back to the closest place to get a tire—Flagstaff, Arizona. Actually, they had to get one from Phoenix so the whole process took quite a while. After a day's delay, we finally got back on the road and made it all the way to Albuquerque, New Mexico, before the axle on the trailer broke. We spent the next three days camped in a 7-Eleven parking lot and got to know the folks from all the shifts on a first-name basis. We became the main topic of neighborhood conversation and I'm sure that Albuquerque has a whole new definition of "boat people" now. The rest of the trip was uneventful except for returning the "loaner" vehicle. I'm pretty sure that employees at that dealership now not only have to pass a drug test but a geography test as well.

We had gained quite a bit of confidence as boaters on our Lake Powell adventure but were still having trouble finding Texas friends willing to trust us. The university where my husband taught had just hired a new choral director. He arrived in the late summer with his children while his wife tied up loose ends at their former home. They weren't used to the heat, so we agreed to take them out on the boat for an afternoon picnic. We were the last boat off the lake as the sun was setting. "The" started right up but went only a couple of feet before she died. This process was repeated over and over until we began to realize that unless we could get the boat to run, we would never reach the far shore and the boat ramp. My husband and son worked on the engine while the new choral teacher and I tied ropes to the bow of the boat and began to swim, pulling the boat very slowly through the water. We figured that at the rate we were going, we might reach the far shore by midnight. Each time the motor would begin to run, my husband would cut it back so we could climb aboard, but before we could accomplish the feat, it would die again. After several tries, the choral teacher and I told them to just go ahead and go as far as they could. We could swim a lot farther if we didn't have to pull the boat. The next time they got the motor going, instead of letting loose and letting them go, we each grabbed opposite sides of the bow and hung on. Our combined weight kept the bow low in the water and, unfortunately for us, the motor kept going this time. While our heads were above the water line, they were in the bow wave and if the prospect of drowning seemed grim, letting go and getting chewed up by the propeller was even grimmer. I looked up through the water to see the kids standing on the deck peering down at me and I wondered if the cartoons of my youth were correct in that the little bubbles I sent up were actually bursting at the surface with squeaky little pleas of "help." Just shy of drowning, we were discovered and the boat turned off so we could be hauled aboard.

It was soon after this adventure that we decided to sell "The" boat. We had done all the repairs to both boat and trailer and had roughly the same amount of money in it as a new boat. We decided horses might be a better recreational pursuit. (Refer to the chapter on horses, if you missed it, to see how that worked.)

> *I looked up through the water to see the kids standing on the deck peering down at me and I wondered if the cartoons of my youth were correct in that the little bubbles I sent up were actually bursting at the surface with squeaky little pleas of "help."*

Years later we moved to California and my brother invited us to spend Thanksgiving on Lake Mohave on a fifty-two-foot houseboat. Our kids joined us and we were off on another great boating adventure. At least this time it was someone else's boat so what could possibly go wrong, right? Wrong! For starters, the weather was chilly and we spent the first night at the marina waiting for first light when we could be piloted out of the marina. Once out of the protection of the cove, we were apprehensive about continuing since the waves were huge. The marina pilot assured us we would be fine once we got going as the wind was to our backs and there were many coves we could duck into if it got any worse. By the afternoon of the first day on the lake, the winds were howling. We radioed back to the marina to ask for help. They told us to find a protecting cove as the winds had now reached hurricane force and there was no way they could get to us … besides, their docks were breaking apart and they were having to cut the rest of their boats loose to drift. Great!

We found a cove that had a high cliff to protect us from the wind but there was no beach. There was, however, a large steel I-beam sticking out from the cliff. We decided to try tying up to that. Before we could accomplish that, the wind caught the back of the boat and swung it around until we found ourselves impaled on the I-beam. Now what? By nightfall we had managed to get free of the I-beam and find a more suitable cove. We spent a very wakeful night hoping the moorings would hold and by morning the winds had died down to a respectable gale.

We had been instructed to head down the lake to another marina as we had lost one of our two engines. We would be running with the wind. When we finally arrived at the marina, they sent out a pilot boat. It tied up to us side by side as they could not steer the silly thing any better than we could. Besides, the wind was still blowing like crazy. My brother went into the office to check out and I watched closely as he came out to try and determine the extent of our indebtedness. I couldn't get a read on what had happened until he got closer and I saw the twinkle in his eye. It seems he chastised them for sending us out in such dangerous weather and told them our vacation had been ruined. Instead of having to pay damages, they gave him another free week for the next season! That being the bright spot of our boating experience, we decided to leave it at that and have stuck to paddles and oars ever since.

Chapter 16

Turnabout's Fair Play—Isn't It?

I don't know who coined the phrase "practical joke," but in my experience I haven't found too many of them to be very practical. I can't remember the very first practical joke I was involved in, but I do know that by the time I was in high school I was becoming rather adept. Perhaps my inspiration came from an aunt a few years older than myself who prided herself on giving just enough information on any given topic to leave me suspended between disbelief and terror. Or perhaps it was my junior high teachers who would send unsuspecting and rather naïve students all over the school searching for things like skyhooks or left-handed monkey wrenches.

My senior year in high school I went to a boarding school and sharpened my skills on my poor, innocent roommate. By the time I reached college, I had risen to the level of "master" in the ranks of practical jokers. They were not always successful, like when another girl and I tried to stuff "a friend" down the laundry chute. She turned out to be a farm girl with amazing strength and knocked our heads together so hard that it took us awhile to remember what we were doing sitting on the floor looking at each other.

I started out in an overflow apartment complex, but it wasn't long until the head dean deemed it wise to move me to the main dorm where she could keep a closer eye on me. That actually increased the victim potential to delightful proportions and kept me occupied with all kinds of projects.

Chapter 16 Turnabout's Fair Play—Isn't It?

From the usual doorknob tricks and harassing people in their sleep, I took on more involved projects like taking apart old nylons (lots and lots of old nylons) and rigging an intricate web through an entire corridor late one night or putting clear wrap under the toilet seats in the rest rooms.

Actually, these pursuits kept me from getting into any serious trouble, so I was somewhat mystified when toward the end of my first year in college I received a letter from the academic dean stating that he didn't think I was very serious about college and maybe I should think about doing something else next year. Sure, my grades weren't stellar, but I had passed most all of my classes ... besides, I really hadn't much cared for those couple of classes that appeared on the surface to be failures.

After some intense negotiations, I returned the next year much more serious and dedicated to my studies. Besides, having a serious relationship with a guy that seemed like someone I could spend the rest of my life with helped a lot. He turned out to be that guy and as we were leaving school to finalize on wedding plans, the wife of the chairman of the music department pulled me aside and said, "Look, I know how you like to play pranks on people but let me give you some advice. You're going to live with this man a very, very long time and you'd better retire any thoughts you might have about playing pranks on him because he *will* get even—over and over and over again. I know this from experience because I can't begin to count the number of cold showers I've had over the years. Just because I dumped a bucket of cold water over the shower curtain onto my husband on our honeymoon!"

Well, no one calls me "sunny" because I'm so bright, but then I'm not especially dull either. I decided to turn in my practical joker's membership card. I have to say it was probably one of the more intelligent decisions I've made, but even so I made a serious error. As my husband and I had children, we would regale them with stories of our youth and as they grew, they began to take on some of our traits from the past.

We had recently bought our retirement home in northern Idaho. While my husband still had another year and a half to teach, I was free to stay in Idaho and take care of a few essential homestead repairs. A major problem was that we only had one car available and my husband needed that to get back to school. So, we loaded up the pantry, kissed each other goodbye and I tried desperately not to cry as I waved until he disappeared through the trees. Thus began a very lonely vigil spent in hard labor during the day while evenings found me hunkered around the phone waiting to hear an encouraging word from the love of my life.

One of the jobs that we needed help with was re-graveling the driveway. Our driveway was quite long, so the trucks were in and out for several days. The gravel guys were concerned about me being all alone and so far out in the boonies without a car. I assured them I'd be fine and they soon finished their job, packed up their equipment and left.

A couple of days later, I received a phone call from the county road commission office's Mr. Berry. He informed me that I would have to come into town right away to settle the tax fee on our newly-graveled driveway. I assured them the work we had done was on private property and that no county road tax should apply. Right away this Mr. Berry guy started asking for my husband. He wanted to know where he was and when he was coming back. I was becoming uncomfortable with his questions and asked to talk to his supervisor. "Ma'am," he emphatically stated, "this is Bill Berry and I am the supervisor." He seemed to know way too much about my situation even bringing up the name of our cat, although he could have been referring to a tractor name. Several more times he asked when my husband would return until I was sure I must be talking to someone who was more interested in that information than any road tax. By the time I hung up I was frightened. Would someone be showing up to rob us or worse?

I walked back and forth across the room for a couple of minutes before deciding I should call my husband. When he answered the phone I started babbling. Before I could finish, Rob, the love of my life, my protector and friend informed me that he had another call coming in and couldn't talk to me just now. He was sure that I'd be all right and perhaps he'd call later. Now my imagination really kicked in. At some later date someone might take enough interest in finding out why I no longer answered my phone only to find a grisly scene and the place stripped bare.

> *Now my imagination really kicked in. At some later date someone might take enough interest in finding out why I no longer answered my phone only to find a grisly scene and the place stripped bare.*

I was next to tears when the phone rang. It was our oldest son. Before he could say much more than "Hi" I was off and running with the story, the words fairly tumbling out. I finally slowed down enough for him to ask, "Who did you say called? A Mr. Berry? Would that be Bill Berry from Bonners Ferry?" Oh, brother! I had been a victim of a not-so-very practical joke! It turns out that our son's father-in-law, uncle and he had a lull in their day's work and cooked up this idea all by themselves. The disguised voice of the uncle kept me from having a clue. They had called my husband immediately after I hung up on them and he agreed to "put me off" until they had finished their prank.

So, it turns out that at least one of our offspring had listened to the tales of my youth a little too closely. I had heard of some of his practical jokes as a teacher but had never thought I would be on the receiving end. As I write this, it is the first day of summer and yesterday was Father's Day. Our oldest son now lives close enough that we were hoping to be able to spend my husband's special day as a father with at least one of our sons and his wife. It turned out that they would not be able to come because of a prior commitment and we swallowed our disappointment and made plans for a childless Father's Day as our other son and his wife live halfway across the country. Early on the evening of the day before Father's Day, our oldest son called to verify some information he needed and told us that his truck was having some problems so that it was just as well that they weren't trying to make the five hour trip to see us. Late that same evening we were up watching a DVD when I thought I heard someone coming into our place. We live in an isolated meadow up in the mountains far from any neighbors and when I saw no lights and couldn't hear anything more, I simply dismissed the idea that I had heard anything at all. Our dog, however, started to growl and then bark loudly. As my husband and I got up to see what was going on, we heard a deep humph sound just outside the door. We had seen a large black bear with her cub across the meadow the week before and thought it might be wise to get the gun before opening the door. The next sound we heard, however, was more of a soft bark and then a whine so we were pretty sure it wasn't a bear after all and opened the door. Besides, by now the dog was wagging his tail and could hardly contain himself. Sure enough, when we looked outside, there stood our son and daughter-in-law with big grins on their faces. "Happy Father's Day!" they both exclaimed. Ah, it was going to be a great day after all!

So, it seems that some practical jokes, as it turns out, are practical after all.

Figure **11**: *So, is she scratching her backside or getting the kinks out of her neck?*

Chapter 17
Tales from a Kitchen

As a youth, I was never actually invited into the kitchen except to get stuff to set the table or clean up. I was not that curious anyway and was content to mow yards, weed gardens and paint either our garage or wood fence every summer. There came a time when I was in high school that my mom was in the hospital and my dad asked me to make tomato soup for the younger kids and himself. Up until that time, toast and cold cereal were the only food items I had any relationship with besides fresh fruit. It turned out that what he asked for was tomato soup and what he expected was cream of tomato soup. A small thing, perhaps, but it turned out to be a pretty big deal. Now, I not only had no interest, but I had no confidence either.

I became engaged in the fall of my sophomore year in college and my aunt, who lived not far from town, invited my fiancé and his family for Thanksgiving dinner. I thought that was really nice until I discovered that she intended for me to cook the entire meal—bread and all. She said if I was going to get married, I should at least have a casual acquaintance with the kitchen. Talk about trial by fire. She helped me plan a menu and saw to it that I had recipes for everything, then walked out of my life for the rest of the day. No one got sick or died and today I have a spoon holder in my kitchen that says, "Many people have eaten my cooking and gone on to live normal lives."

Later on, during that same school year, my fiancé invited me to his home to study. I really didn't have much to study and since his mom was not yet home from work, he suggested that I might busy myself in the kitchen. I could make him a cherry pie while he studied. Yikes! I didn't have a clue how to make a cherry pie—or any other kind of pie for that matter. I knew I had to come up with some excuse pretty quickly if I didn't want to expose my ignorance.

> *I became engaged in the fall of my sophomore year in college and my aunt, who lived not far from town, invited my fiancé and his family for Thanksgiving dinner. I thought that was really nice until I discovered that she intended for me to cook the entire meal—bread and all.*

First, I tried the "most women are proprietary about their kitchens and don't want someone else messing around in them" ploy. My fiancé assured me that his mom wasn't like that and wouldn't mind at all coming home to a fresh baked pie. Next, I told him that I would need a recipe for crust and I was sure his mom wouldn't have one as she probably had it in her head. He left his studies, came out into the kitchen and rummaged around until he found a recipe. Lastly, I assured him that they probably didn't have the prerequisite ingredients for a cherry pie and that maybe I had some studying to do after all. Not wanting to give up on the idea of pie for dessert, he came back out into the kitchen and dug out everything I would need. Rats! Oh well, I could read, how hard could it be?

I mixed the crust and tried to roll it out but, try as I might, I could not get the silly stuff to stick together enough to get it into the pan. Finally, next to tears, I came out to confess I really didn't know how to make a pie. I buried my effort at crust near the bottom of the trash, cleaned up the kitchen (at least I knew how to do that) and was just headed for the living room when I heard my prospective mother-in-law return home. She was greeted by her son with, "Hi, Mom. Can you teach CJ how to make a pie?" *Groan*. Now she was sure to have second thoughts about sending her son off with a wife that didn't even know how to make a pie. The old song about "Billy Boy" came to mind. Well, she made me dig my "attempt" out of the trash, analyzed it and declared it to only lack a bit more water. She whipped out a new crust, threw the pie together and left me to wonder just what "a bit" was.

I didn't have time to get embarrassed over cooking again until after our wedding. We were on our honeymoon when my husband asked me to make him some chocolate pudding. Actually, anything other than my proven menu of cold cereal would have been a challenge but once again I figured, "How hard can it be?" The directions said medium heat and, to be on the safe side, I kicked it down a notch. I think it was about an hour and a cramped arm muscle later that we finally sat down to eat our chocolate pudding. This whole cooking thing was turning out to be a lot more complicated than I figured.

Gradually I did improve and other than a pumpkin pie that I forgot to put the sugar in, (you don't ever want to try that—yuck!) life in the kitchen was progressing rather nicely. I simply avoided pies and my reading skills seemed to suffice in most other areas of cooking.

I finally found a crust recipe that I felt was fail-safe and began to rather enjoy being able to release my artistic endeavors on designing the top crust. One day, a number of years into our marriage, we received a call from the principal's wife saying that a friend whom several of us had formerly taught with would be passing through on his way to look at another job. He would stop at our school for a short visit. The principal's wife thought it would be fun to pool our resources and all eat together for a nice noon meal. The day before our friend was to arrive, two of the families came down with some kind of bug. The day of our friend's arrival, something came up that the principal's family had a noon conflict. That left me to prepare the entire meal, including dessert, a lemon meringue pie that it seems our friend had rather strongly requested. It certainly wasn't my dessert of choice, although I liked eating it well enough. First came the crust to be prebaked before adding the lemon filling. Horror of horrors, when I went to take it out it was like a small frisbee lying peacefully on the bottom of the pan. I tried the other crust since my recipe made two crusts. It shrank also. I must have left something out, so I quickly mixed up two more crusts. I stationed my husband in front of the little oven window and asked him to watch it for me. For each of the next two crusts I heard him exclaim, "There she goes!" Time was getting short. This time I used a different recipe and frantically mixed up two more crusts. Both of those were frisbee-like as well. I was now out of time. I quickly put together the lemon filling, but what to do about the meringue? Meringue needs something to hold on to, preferably a crust, or it will shrink. I added the meringue to the lemon filling and popped it into the oven to brown, full well knowing it would end up looking like a too-small clown hat on top. Oh well, this would just have to do.

Our guest arrived and we had a good time right up until dessert. He rubbed his hands together, smacked his lips and said, "Oh, boy, I know we're having lemon meringue pie for dessert and I can hardly wait." That doesn't sound so bad, but I knew this guy pretty well and I was never going to hear the end of this, so I just went ahead and "fessed up." "We're not having lemon meringue pie today. It's a new kind of lemon dessert. You just put one of these frisbee things on your plate, spoon some lemon and topping on and just eat it. It tastes just like lemon meringue pie so I don't want to hear any more about it."

Unfortunately, I was to hear a lot more about it because our friend didn't take the job he came to look at … he came to our school. We would be on a music tour with the kids from school and our friend would walk up to a complete stranger and introduce himself. Then he would turn to me and say, "This is my friend, Mrs. Anderson, and she makes the most unusual pies." I would always reward his efforts with an extremely blushed face as he would proceed to tell about my "frisbee pie."

One day, I decided to bake another lemon meringue pie. I had never had any more trouble with crusts and thought if this one turned out especially well, I might even invite our friend over. As it turned out, Betty Crocker would have been pleased to feature that pie in any of her cookbooks. It was absolutely stunning to behold and held good promise that it would taste sublime as well.

I called our friend and asked him to come over right away, if possible. I had something really important to discuss with him. When the doorbell rang a few minutes later, I silently ushered our friend into the kitchen, swung open the cupboard door with a dramatic, "Ta-da!" then slammed it shut again with the declaration, "And you're not getting one stinking bite either!" The ensuing dialog went something like this.

Him: "Surely we can work something out?"

Me: "For a piece of this pie, I don't ever want to hear any more embarrassing comments about my pies."

Him: "I'm pretty sure that would take the whole pie."

Me: "I'm pretty sure one piece will do or you'll not get any at all."

Him: "Well then, I'm pretty sure I have just enough time before my next class to eat that piece."

So, he sat down and ate his piece of pie all the while smacking his lips and declaring it to be the very best pie he had ever eaten. So, I thought that would be the end of it. The very next time we were on a tour, he sidled up to the nearest stranger, introduced himself first, then me and said, "Have I ever told you about Mrs. Anderson's unusual pies?" I couldn't believe what I was hearing. "Well, I'm awfully sorry, but I can't tell you," he said as he turned and walked away, leaving me to try and explain the whole sorry story to a perfect stranger.

It was many months after the frisbee incident that I learned that any pie crust recipe will do the shrinking thing if the gluten content in the flour is too high. Today, I make wonderful pies (if you ask me) and have even managed to gain a degree of confidence in the kitchen.

Chapter 18
A Song for Your Heart

To be more like Jesus is the hope of my heart. To do His will and live for Him is my quest. May the words of this song encourage you in your quest to be more like Jesus and may the tune help you remember that Jesus is the melody in the song of life!

Chapter 18 A Song for Your Heart 109

Conclusion

Life is an adventure! God is Awesome and loves you like no one else can! Let Him be your constant Companion and Friend and together you'll find life to be quite an incredible ride!

Fine
(the end)

TEACH Services, Inc.
P U B L I S H I N G

We invite you to view the complete
selection of titles we publish at:
www.TEACHServices.com

We encourage you to write us
with your thoughts about this,
or any other book we publish at:
info@TEACHServices.com

TEACH Services' titles may be purchased in
bulk quantities for educational, fund-raising,
business, or promotional use.
bulksales@TEACHServices.com

Finally, if you are interested in seeing
your own book in print, please contact us at:
publishing@TEACHServices.com

We are happy to review your manuscript at no charge.

www.ingramcontent.com/pod-product-compliance
Lightning Source LLC
Chambersburg PA
CBHW070557160426
43199CB00014B/2536